Teaching Students with Autism Spectrum Disorder in the Early Childhood Classroom:
a guidebook for parents and new teachers

by

Stephanie L. Lindner

Printed in the United States of America

First Printing, 2023

ISBN 979-8-218-28368-1

Independently Published

DEDICATION

I dedicate this book to my former students, who were some of my best teachers, and to the many children being diagnosed with autism spectrum disorder every day. May this book support those who will contribute to your educational journey.

Stephanie L. Lindner

CONTENTS

Stephanie L. Lindner

Acknowledgments

I want to thank my former students, and all the colleagues that I worked with at Yonkers Public Schools, New York City Department of Education, and New Milford Public Schools. Your support has helped me become the teacher I am today.

I want to thank my family, my husband Jared, and Uncle Alex for believing in me and pushing me to keep writing.

I want to thank my son Bret for giving me the love and strength that I need to be the best version of myself.

Foreword

As soon as I graduated with a B.A. in English Literature, I started working with students as a Teacher's Assistant. I had my own resource room where I would pull students who were struggling out of class and work on targeted skills for grades K-8th grade. Afterward, I worked in a nursery school assisting children ages 2-4 years old. Then, I worked in a 2nd grade ICT (Inclusive Classroom Teaching) Classroom. I was a student teacher for a classroom with a 6:1:1 ratio, with students with multiple disabilities and a classroom teacher for a class with a 12:1:1 ratio with students who had multiple disabilities.

I graduated from a dual-master's program in special education and early childhood education. Nothing I studied in college, could have prepared me from what I learned in the classroom on my own. The best learning came from the students themselves. They were the best teachers. Reading a textbook could give you some pointers that may or may not work.

The first year of teaching in a special education classroom gave me my hardest but best lessons. As each year went by, I learned more and more how to teach students with disabilities. I started writing down things I learned, and what my colleagues would tell me so I would have it all in one place for reference, a sort of guidebook to myself.

Overall, I have had a lot of success in my classroom. With effort, you can help teach a student self-control to manage meltdowns and outbursts, and how to read and move on to a less restrictive environment. Seeing a student make progress doesn't happen overnight, and there's no one magic solution. The best strategies take consistency, effort, and time before you'll be able to see any progress, but when you do, it's one of the most priceless feelings in the world.

My aim and sole purpose for this book is to help parents and new teachers with a general guide to different aspects of teaching students with autism in the classroom. Before we begin, let me explain that this is a guidebook based on the strategies that I have personally tried in my years of experience teaching in multiple settings with children who have multiple disabilities. The strategies that I share are because I have directly enforced them or have observed them working for myself. It is important that you understand that what I share in this book, may not work for every single child with autism. It is important that you understand that these are my opinions that are based on my experiences and you have a right to disagree. To protect the identity of students, I have chosen to omit their names; however, I feel confident that you will take something out of it that you *can* use to support students with disabilities.

This guidebook started as a guide to myself, but as I started adding more and more pieces of information, I felt like parents can use it as well as a reference. I worked as a coach for new teachers and a lot of what I wrote in this book I have shared with my Student Teachers. In my experience, parents of children with autism often feel like they are alone. New teachers feel like they are like the proverbial fish out of water. I know I did.

In my first year of teaching students with multiple disabilities, I felt vastly unprepared. I was a decent student. My cumulative GPA was a 3.8. I certainly was well read, to say the least, but on my first day of school, I felt completely clueless. I remember being surrounded by my new colleagues and the first five minutes I had to help a student with Oppositional Defiance Disorder who was also mentally disturbed and had autism. He was having a severe meltdown. He could not sit in his chair to eat breakfast. He was screaming and crying. I felt powerless. I did not know what to do. All I could do was try my best to help him sit down so he would stop squirming on the floor. Upon reading my students' IEP's (Individualized Education Plans), I came to realize that 10 out of 12 were categorized as emotionally disturbed, had Oppositional Defiance Disorder, Autism, and Attention Deficit Hyperactivity Disorder (ADHD).

In the classroom, I faced challenging obstacles with students and colleagues alike. When a student would have a meltdown to the point where he would cause himself or others' harm, most of the time I was alone. The security guards in my school refused to help me. Not once did anyone help me. There was no crisis management team. I sometimes had paraprofessionals who did not want to be responsible for helping the kids during their meltdowns so they would not assist me either.

During my observations, my room could be chaotic. I had to be in twelve different places at once while also trying to teach and differentiate a lesson and delegate directions to my paraprofessionals. The second I would step away from one student, another would be trying to climb up the top of the closet. It was a tough time, but when students can learn to trust you, they are able to learn and have rewarding experiences that will help them in their lives. I spent twenty minutes in total for the entire year with a teacher who was supposed to be my mentor. I collaborated with occupational therapists, speech therapists, and physical therapists on a weekly basis. A lot of what I learned over time through trial and error, I was able to incorporate into my daily routine with my students.

Let us begin by talking about those strategies, and how to teach students with autism and multiple disabilities. Students with autism need boundaries just like any child, but they also need accommodations and modifications to set them up for success. We will review real-life scenarios, and cover different topics such as academic, behavior, assessments, collaboration with therapists and parents.

Chapter 1: Sensory Therapy

All students need sensory breaks, regardless of whether they are on the spectrum. I, for one, can barely sit down for a long period of time; I need to get up and move around. In general, sometimes getting up and using the bathroom can be a break enough for adults, stretching for five minutes, browsing social media, or opening your emergency snack drawer and selecting your cheat fix. Whatever it is, we tend to find excuses to take a short break and move our bodies. Students with autism should be given an opportunity to do this as well. So it's imperative that you are flexible enough to end a lesson early to allow for transition time, but also a short **Sensory Break**.

Sensory breaks were a part of the routine I established because students needed it every day. I taught in what is considered to be a specialized class with a ratio of 12:1. In an Inclusion Class, you may find it harder to stray from your schedule because you're afraid you'll "lose" your kids' attention. Try to keep an open mind, set an analog timer, or find a virtual one and keep it up on the smartboard with a countdown. Let students know, "We are taking a short sensory break and when you hear the alarm go off, we're going to begin math." For me, sometimes it is not the sensory break itself but finding the right time to implement it that is the tricky part. Sensory breaks help my students essentially take a break. Depending on the sensory break, it can help the student get some energy out, relax, and help regulate emotions. With students who are on the autism spectrum, sensory breaks should be considered as part of their learning. When you learn something new, your physical needs have to be met, otherwise this can deter students from focusing on you.

Model First – What You Want Students To Learn

In general, everything will need to be modeled to students if you want them to do it right. This goes for academics, social-emotional behavior, and sensory breaks too. Show them and teach them because anyone can tell someone what to do. You have to show what is the expected behavior, and how the sensory break should look, sound, and feel.

- Will they need to stand up out of their seat?
- Will they need to sit down?

Show your kids what you want them to do before you ask them to do it. Modeling should be the rule of thumb for everything in general education and in special education. Children need to be shown what to do, not just told what to do, and they'll also need opportunities to practice it in order for a skill to be mastered or generalized into different settings.

For example, I used to tell my students, "Please,

don't cut each other in line" every day and I sounded like a broken record, as the expression goes. I showed them "Stop. Go" Walk in Line visuals, a red stop sign for—stop, and a green traffic light for—go. We listened to stories about being a good citizen, a good friend, and we engaged in conversation. It wasn't until I added a little humor, a little drama, and had a student volunteer to line up at the door to model that they understood. I got up, ran, and deliberately cut the student. The student looked at me quizzically while smirking; it seemed like he knew I was not being serious. Other students laughed at how eagerly I got up and cut the student. I asked, "Was that nice? What I just did? Is it nice to cut someone when you're lining up?" A few kids chorally said, "No" followed by a look of disappointment. Then I walked behind the student and said, "This is where I go. I go right behind the person in front of me."

I showed them again and asked for kids to have a turn and show me. I stepped aside. Four students got up and looked back at me adorably as they attempted to cut the person in front of them. Some of them went behind the child in front of them and frowned, folding their arms feeling sad they were not first in line. We practiced this several times. Expect to practice this as a whole group once or twice before transitioning outside the classroom. Then, when students have mastered it, you won't have to practice as much, and you can gradually fade prompts.

If a student is reluctant to start a "hands on" activity, model it first and provide the necessary prompts (physical, visual, verbal). I was excited to test out child smocks that were gifted by a donor. My students were painting and I handed out the smocks so they could wear it on top of their clothes. One student was afraid to put the smock over his head. I was verbally prompting him that he had nothing to be afraid of and then managed to put it over my head. Of course, he did not need to put the smock on, but I'm sure his mother was happy that he did.

When Should Students Take a Sensory Break

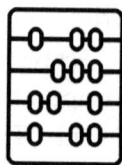

A sensory break can be three to five-minute intervals in between lessons, or after a 50-minute period. If you are transitioning between subjects such as math into reading or vice versa, you may want to do a quick sensory break for the students to regroup and refocus.

Why Are Sensory Breaks Important?

Breaks help with refocusing and behavior management. It eases frustration. It's also a transitional tool. Students with autism tend to seek out sensory experiences. Sitting down for a long period of time to work is not realistic. I find that providing opportunities can help ease their frustration and increase motivation throughout the academic routine. Students look forward to them, and sensory breaks also make learning fun and rewarding. Some examples that have worked for me are: engaging in facilitated yoga exercises, guided dance routines, center tables with various sensory play bins that have different textures (sand, rice, Play-Doh, pasta, beans, etc.) paired with small tools (shovel, pail, beginner chopsticks, clamps, etc.) If you have center tables, set a timer and rotate students or the centers themselves, so everyone can get a chance to engage in the different experiences.

As the school year progresses, you will have learned more about your students' personalities, their interests, and capabilities. If you are a parent reading this book to help you with your child, then you have the advantage of using your prior knowledge and experience. As teachers, we have the student's Individualized Education Plan (IEP)to guide us. Connecting with parents can also give you more information that is probably not included in the plan. As you make your observations, write anecdotes. Then, you will start to notice if John tends to get frustrated after lunch, or if he is triggered by whole group instruction during a specific time. With daily observations, you will be able to tell when your students are restless. Ask parents questions and show that you are interested in their child.

When you read a student's IEP, you would have learned a lot about his/her behavior and get a good sense of where the student is academically, socially, and physically. However, having a parent conference is a great start to building a collaborative and supportive relationship. I suggest you write down your questions before your introductory parent conference, but after you read the IEP. Then take notes. You can ask "What does John like to do for fun? What goals do you have for John this school year (academic and social), Does John like working for anything at home? What are some things he is interested in? What is his favorite snack? Does he have any allergies?"

Learning about John will help you, as a teacher, support him in learning. If John likes trains, maybe you could read a book about trains and work on some of his academic goals in the process. Perhaps, you have a few toys and one of them is a train, John can work to play with the train for several minutes as a reward, in turn for completing age-appropriate academic activities. Perhaps the IEP states, "John likes to engage in sensory-based activities, that include sand, Play-Doh, or rice."

Meanwhile in class, John just finished completing file folder activities, where he had to sequence numbers from 0-10. John is starting to get tired and uninterested in the numbers. He seems ready to move on to the next subject. What I do is give John the reward such as a sticker, or points on his behavior management system. Then give John Play-Doh accompanied with tools with Play-Doh mats related to the next subject. Set a timer to let John know when the sensory break will end, and prompt him when its closer to ending, then clean up and move onto the next subject. John is able to roll, squeeze, cut, etc. I allow John some uninterrupted quiet meditative time for sensory play. Usually, the students are quiet and focused. The timer soon goes off, and I sing our clean up song as soon as the timer starts ringing. I model cleaning up. John follows and gathers all the Play-Doh into the cup, then puts the tools in the tool bin. The kids get sanitizer then we transition into the next subject.

I can tell when students need a sensory break, as they will appear to show signs of frustration. If the repetitive behaviors are interrupting the class, or home activities, then consider taking several breaks after every period, or a few longer breaks instead for that day. Just because they appear to be frustrated, it does not mean they psychologically feel that way; it may be a physical thing and what the body needs. Keep in mind there is no singular way to engage in a sensory break, it can be fast or slow.

Sensory breaks can be yoga, meditation techniques such as facilitated long and deep breaths, followed by wait time. Breaks can be dancing, simple stretches, and body movement provided with a model that students can follow easily one step at a time. Putting on a guided dance on the internet may work for some children. Others may need a model or an actual person in front of them, and/or visuals of the movements e.g., showing a picture of raised hands or clapping. You can also prompt verbally , e.g. "Hands up. Now, clap your hands like this." Just because they do not engage in dancing does not automatically mean they are disinterested. Everything needs to be taught and modeled. Once they get the hang of how it goes, then it becomes easier. Dancing needs to be modeled step-by-step! You need to be motivated about the dance too. When you buy a fitness program, does the instructor seem motivated? Does he/she inspire you? Or are they withdrawn and bored?

Something to keep in mind is to give a sensory break that the child can easily follow, then later on as the school year progresses, you can move into more complicated breaks. If the dance is too complex in the beginning, the child may get frustrated, sit down, and give up. For example, you may want to just focus on moving side to side for the first week. Once, they've mastered that then move on to the second step. Go with the flow!

Sensory Breaks and Possible Hinderances

Perhaps, the student does not want to engage in the sensory break, although he/she usually does. The child can be experiencing multiple things at once such as a lack of sleep, lack of food, dehydration, or a personal family matter, to name a few. Poor diet and nutrition inhibits our ability to focus. Having a healthy diet, good sleep, and an exercise routine makes us feel like

we can put our best foot forward. You can encourage the student to engage in a sensory break, but you feel he/she needs one you can integrate your rewards system. You can say something like "If you do ____, you will get a sticker." It doesn't have to be a sticker per say, you can use an activity that the child likes such as coloring time, computer time, two pretzel chips, etc." Create a communication board where you can provide a visual example of the choices in an organized way.

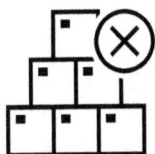

Keep Sensory Breaks As Part Of Daily Routines

Teaching in an inner-city school, most of my students were from low-income neighborhood, and consequently our school had very little resources. We did not have our own gym, art, or music room. Going outside was complicated because we shared a building with a second school. Scheduling a time to go out meant you had to not only talk with your supervisors, but the staff in the other school as well. Naturally, when there are too many people sharing a space, tension rises.

Most of the time, I got a run around and my supervisors did not want to have any reason to speak to the other school. My kids were lucky to go out five times per month. Once we got outside, the students could walk around and play hopscotch or run. We didn't have any outdoor equipment for them to use unless we decided to spend our own money. Sensory breaks in the classroom were essential because we had nowhere to go.

Our everyday routine is as follows: By the end of our second academic period, we take a sensory break for several minutes. Each academic period is fifty minutes. First, we do a series of stretches where we count from 1-10 in Spanish. Introducing a new language to students helps add to a sense of cultural mindfulness in the classroom. If you want the student to learn a new language, this will be a great time to introduce it. I incorporate jumping jacks, jump in place, and crisscross feet, run in place, and a few other stretches. Each exercise goes on for 10 seconds. Then the students look and listen to a guided dance for one to three minutes each song. Some days, we do three songs and some days four or more depending on if I feel they need extended exercise.

The kids like routine and can choose the same three songs for the entire year if I let them. If I am not sure which song to choose, I will ask, "Does anyone have a suggestion?" Several students will raise their hand. I taught my students to raise their hand whilst using their other hand to put their finger over their mouth. This will help them to learn that I will call on them and give them attention if they are displaying the desired behavior, which is being quiet and raising their hand. If all students make the habit of calling out then it is very hard to hear anyone's suggestion, much less conduct an orderly activity and provide a sense of safety. That is when students will shout over others to make sure you hear them. As a result, the shouting can trigger a student who may be hypersensitive to loud noises. Then, suddenly the situation escalates.

We need to prevent things like that from happening to make sure everyone has fun safely. I say, "Who has a suggestion? I am only taking those who are raising their hands." Then, I'll give them a visual prompt, through picture or by modeling it myself. "If you are calling out, I cannot call on you," I'll repeat again. I had several students who tended to call out, shout, and cry if you did not choose them. I repeated this way and did not call them until they raised their hand quietly for the next round. If a student cries, tell them why you didn't pick them and mention that there is another opportunity either later in the day or tomorrow and they can try again. Repeat verbal reminders as they are needed.

Sensory Therapy and the Use of Vibration in Therapy Tools

I had submitted a project through a donation website which offers resources to teachers. If it were not for donors, I could not have afforded resources for my students and office supplies. I spend hundreds of dollars on my students and every year, I continued to spend more of my own money with each year I worked in the city. Teachers don't live extravagant lives, but we do it

because we want to and we aren't given tools otherwise. Through this website, I had listed several items which would service the students, chosen from an organization that specializes in creating sensory toys and devices. One these was a vibrating bendable soft/ texturized rod that the kids called "Snakey." Snakey did not have any face, and actually he did not look like a snake at all except for his long, bendable, blue body. However, the name stuck, and a star was born. There are three settings for Snakey, from low to high vibration or off. Before students use Snakey, they wash/ and or sanitize their hands. After each use, I take an antibacterial wipe and wipe Snakey.

During busing, our classrooms would all switch. Each classroom was assigned a bus number. The students that were assigned that bus had to go to the designated room. I would have a new set of students for dismissal. I would have a mix of students in grades K-5. I noticed that even the older students liked Snakey. They would often request him to massage their head for several minutes at a time. It would prevent any nonpreferred behaviors from happening. The vibrations seemed to soothe and calm students.

I could see Snakey was good at promoting self-regulation and re-directing actions. There is a wide variety of battery-operated vibrating therapy toys for kids including stuffed animals that are soft and cuddly. The kids can squeeze and turn the vibrations on or off when they want. Before giving battery-operated toys to my students, I make sure the battery door is closed. I may even put a piece of thick tape over the hatch to keep it more secured and safer.

I found vibrating pens at a school supply store. After buying one or two, I observed some students rubbing the pen all over their arms or faces. When this happens, I verbally prompt and model how to use a pen appropriately on paper. It occurs to me that with these particular students, the need for vibration and sensory input is strong. Aside from helping their hand stretch and making marks on paper, the students were practically obsessed with the vibrations. The pen was a small tool, easily controlled and fun to use, but with anything, an adult should always monitor and model the use of anything, even a pen.

Sensory Cushions

As part of providing physical accommodations to students in the classroom, I've utilized one inflatable disc cushion and one bagel cushion. In my first year, I got a semi-broken disc cushion from an occupational therapist since most of my students were going to be seen by this person. After using some duct tape, I could still use the cushion and rotate it to the students that needed it. I made the mistake in not monitoring or modeling first to my students on how to use the cushion properly. As they used the cushion for the first few times, it quickly popped and deflated. I was too busy teaching lessons, but when you are a teacher, you must do several things at once and your eyes have to be all over the classroom, so to speak.

For the cushions, a regular basketball pump can be used to blow them up. Be mindful of letting the right amount of air in to provide enough buoyancy. Too much air is bad, and too little is also bad. Cushions can be purchased online via internet search. During parent-teacher conferences, I often get asked, *"How do I help him/her sit at the dinner table?"* I bring up the therapy cushions every year, but parents are reluctant to buy it.

Therapy tools for students with autism can be very expensive and it will take some hunting around to find one that is reasonably priced. Like I said before, even teachers struggle with this. Students are lucky to get any toys or physical therapy rooms at school. I honestly think there should be more options in stores and online where parents can buy more affordable therapy toys and devices for students with special needs. With the donor website, I managed to get another cushion after drafting up a proposal and selecting the cushion that I had wanted. It took several weeks for my project to get fully funded, and several more for it to ship. Once I received it, I rotated it amongst the students immediately.

Public school teachers and therapists in the city often find ways to make their own therapy devices, and this takes time and dedication with a touch of creativity. With the help of the occupational therapists, we bounced back ideas to help students with self-regulation. I pulled elastic fitness bands around the front legs of the chair. If you have an old pair of sweatpants with an elastic band, you can pull out the elastic band and tie to each end to the front legs of the student's chair. According to observations, students like to put their feet behind the elastic band and bring it forward with their sneakers. It helps keep their feet back and encourages them to sit for a longer period of time. At any time, they can put their feet in front of the band. Before allowing students to use it, first model. Sit down and put your feet behind the band.

Weighted Vest--How Do You Use It? What Does It Provide For The Child?

The vest provides weight and pressure. It reminds me of when someone gives you a hug--a squeeze-- you feel their weight on you. You feel their warmth and pressure, and the squeeze can be calming. The weighted vest can act as a hug in that sense and help them maintain self-regulation. Whether it's at home or in the classroom, set a timer to remind you of when to take the vest off. I have one weighted vest. This vest can be 1 lb-2 lb. Occupational Therapists that I've worked in tandem with suggest the vest be worn for several minutes at a time. When therapists push in their services into the classroom, the most I've seen them keep it on a child is for 15 minutes. The weight of the vest should be determined by the therapist in conjunction with the child's age, height, weight, and social behavior/ and physical therapy goals. The vest can be found online via internet search. I use the vest on the students who we refer to as "runners," as they'll often run about the classroom to obtain a certain item or elope from a nonpreferred activity.

Students will find reasons to get up, whether it's to play with another student on the opposite side of the room, get a toy, go to the bathroom down the hall, or get water. I had one student who tried getting up to get water five times per 50-minute intervals. The result was that he did not engage in the lesson at all. In this case, I'd use the vest for fifteen minutes while setting a timer. When the timer was up, he was allowed to get up and drink water. I did not want him to miss the learning material during whole group instruction. Analog timers help in providing a visual of how much time is left going from a whole to half then down to a quarter, coupled with verbal prompts, is an effective strategy during activities. I'd show him a visual of a boy sitting in his chair and tell him politely to wait.

Additionally, I shared information on the behavior of my students with their parents. When I brought up the issue of how the student got up to get water every few minutes, the father of the child told me that if I allow this to happen, eventually he will throw up from all the water. He said, "Please do not allow him to do this. Tell him no." In other words, this was a repeated pattern. So, he ended up getting water frequently at home, too. In this case, I continued the timer, and even encouraged the father to bring in a water bottle so I could track his water intake. If the child does not know how to read, then also add a sticker — color code the cups, and inform the student which color is his/hers.

Sensory Tools/ Diet

As directed by an Occupational Therapist, you can use different sensory tools and come up with a sensory diet. A sensory diet incorporates an individual's needs with experiences related to physical senses. As you work in tandem with therapists and the teaching team, you can come up with a sensory diet for your child at home as well. For example, if a student has sensory brushes as part of their diet, the brush is used to brush the skin gently with soft plastic bristles for an allotted time. After each use, wash the brush with soap and water. Every year, the toy and educational supply companies come up with new sensory toys for students. Let me be clear, these toys are for ALL children, and even grownups too. Don't you remember stress balls or beanie balls? You can hold, squeeze, or throw them. Beanie balls were fun to grasp because you controlled where the beans would move. You can make your own beanies with dry rice and/or beans.

In my first year, I bought a variety of fidget toys. The purpose of fidget toys is to relief anxiety/ stress. I bought a variety in my first year. I bought some that looked like a game station controller with several buttons and levers you can press and manipulate. I bought fidget toys that spin and toys with a marble inside mesh where you can move the marble from one end to another. I spent a lot of money getting them; each toy itself was a pretty penny.

The occupational therapist I had worked with in my first year, I'll call him Mr. E, was so savvy at making his own therapy and sensory toys. It was a way to give the students what they needed while saving a few bucks. He would incorporate his creations into his sessions and make sensory toys from stuff found around the house, that the students could use in the classroom and even take home. For example, he would get a clean unused sock and fill it up with materials that the students could squeeze. For my calm down corner, he made the teachers sensory boards which had different textures and toys that students can engage with when they needed a sensory break. He would glue shiny beads, rice, dry beans, pieces of different sample rugs, pipe cleaners with beads, and so forth. This way, when the students walked to the calm down corner, they were allowed to receive sensory input.

For one of my students who was diagnosed with Oppositional Defiance Disorder, he decided to make a transition tool. This student had difficulty with transitioning. This meant moving from one place to another or simply moving on to the next subject like literacy to math. I had rotating centers in place, and my student was expected to move from one table to the next to work on three different activities that were approximately 10-15 minutes long. When he would transition, he would cry and refuse to do any work. The OT therapist decided to help with this issue and weaved it into one of his sessions. He bought an expensive water bottle that morning at the corner deli. I'm sure he enjoyed all the minerals that were in the water. It was a hard plastic bottle. He filled it with water, beads, a few drops of food coloring and oil. It became a homemade sensory toy and worked as a transition tool as well. He took the time to fill it up with glitter and animal shaped beads with one of my students during their session. He used hot glue to glue down the cap.

During our rotating centers, the student took this transition tool with him. It helped calm him down, and his meltdowns were shorter in duration. He called it "The Magic Wand." He loved watching the water and oil go up and down, as beads danced around the container. He was fixated with its movement. When my class would transition, whether it was inside or outside the classroom, he would request the transition tool.

"I need the magic wand."

The magic wand was with him only during transitions and we would put it beside him when he would engage in the center activity. He was discouraged to have it in his hands all day because then he would not have enough time to complete other activities, and it was our belief that he would be less motivated by the transition tool with its overuse.

Transition tools can really be anything that the student can touch. It can be a keychain, phone, fidget toy, or a few pieces of a favorite snack. Transition tools are aimed at helping students self soothe. Students with autism can respectively become anxious during transitions, changes in routine, and anything threatening sameness and security. Sameness is like a wall which they can put their back up against. Sameness allows them to have a baseline ground underneath their feet for an ever-changing world.

Sensory Bins

Sensory bins are stationed at center tables or multi-sensory area in your classroom. I typically buy plastic bins approximately 12x12 with clasps at either side. They can be relatively 3-5 inches deep. In my experience, I find that when students engage in sensory bin activities, their restricted behaviors are less intense, and they're able to redirect their attention. What goes inside the bin is what makes it multi-sensory: materials that students can touch, hear, and that are also aesthetically pleasing as to provide visual stimuli. I have bins filled with kinetic sand. I also have bins with dry rice, dry pasta, beads/ glitter, buckets, sifters, spoons, and dramatic play toys.

Have students wash their hands beforehand. During center stations and/or small group instruction, I will incorporate the sensory bins. Students love to touch, grasp, move, handle different materials to get sensory input if they are constantly seeking to enhance sensory experiences. As students engage in sensory bins, have them work side by side with another student—sharing materials. Working close to another student and/or sharing materials is a great start in providing opportunities for socialization. An adult can facilitate interaction between students by question and answer dialogue. Create symbols that illustrate both the questions, sentence starters and choices. I try to incorporate sensory activities in my lesson in some small way. If I am doing literacy centers, I may put characters from a story that I've laminated, or laminated sight words into the sand or rice bins with Velcro dots on the back instead of toys. Students can find the sight words and match them to the sight words on another laminated sheet. You can also use laminated letters, numbers or if you have magnets or letter/number beads. In the classroom, I will make it one center out of three, then rotate every 10−15 minutes. It gives the students something to look forward to in the academic period.

Don't Forget- Model Everything

How do you use the sand bin? You can go over some rules that you may want to keep in mind, by modeling how you use the bin. Pose the question, "How do we work with the sand? Show students the bin, show them the sand, shovel the sand out of the bin and dump it back in." Verbally prompt students as you show how the sand stays in. For example, show them how to fill up a pail and turn it over to make a sandcastle. You can hunt for the letter A, then pick it up out of the sand and match it on your file folder/ or laminated paper. When introducing a new activity—always model it, and model appropriate behaviors. You can model how to ask to use a certain toy, "Can you please pass the shovel?" in facilitated play. If you accidentally throw the sand out of the bin onto the table, then model and narrate how you would scoop the sand into your hand and put it back in the bin, "Oops! I threw the sand out of the bin, and it fell on top of the table, that's ok. Let me just scoop it back in." Use your best judgement when modeling behavioral norms and activities and make them consistent with house/classroom rules. If at first the child does not feel comfortable using the sand, an adult should model how to play and use the sand toys whilst providing a verbal path illustrating step-by-step thinking, ex. "I can take some sand in my left hand and use my right hand to shape it into this mold." Children should learn what is acceptable and unacceptable in playing with their peers. Be prepared to go over the rules and provide prompts whenever you do the activity.

Chapter 2: Behavior Interventions and Support Systems

There are various behavioral interventions and support systems. You have to find the one that works best for your child and/or students, depending on what is age appropriate and how much you are willing to maintain the system. Finding ways to work it into your classroom routine will take daily practice. Implementing this at the beginning of the school year is crucial for setting the tone for the classroom. These interventions and support systems need to be taught, modeled, and carried out with patience and persistence. In order for them to work, you have to really commit to them and hold them to a high degree of importance. Here are a few strategies that I would recommend:

"First—Then Chart"

A "First—Then" chart is a reward-based strategy for non-preferred activities followed by a preferred activity, which can also serve as a transitional tool toward the next step in a visual schedule. Make a "First—Then" chart with the activity you wish your child to complete in the "First" column, then follow it with a reward "Then." In other words, first they do the non-preferred activity, then

once they complete it they receive the reward, or the preferred activity. You can also make your own by creating a two-box frame table online with a word processor. Then copy and paste pictures that include your child's routine and the rewards that he/she will be interested in.

I find the visuals that work for me are (e.g. "First Write" (picture of student writing), "Then Computer" (picture of student using the computer)"; "First Math" (Picture shows student using blocks to count), "Then Tablet" (Student using the tablet); "First Read" (Student reading a book), "Then Snack (Student eating a snack.) The snack can be from his/her lunch/ or from their snack bag (if they have one.) If you have a snack to give, make sure he/she is not allergic to it. Check their emergency card/ health records/history etc.

I always present a visual with each choice and the word next to, under or on the picture. The "Then" should be something that the child likes. If it is a snack, I recommend something not overly sweet, and small in quantity. The reason is that my students have a lot of sugar or the service providers/ prep teachers provide cookies as a reward early in the morning, then they have an even more challenging time with their thought processing/reasoning as opposed to quick reaction time and impulsivity, and self-control. If the reward is the computer or tablet, I recommend setting an analog timer.

Before you give the child his/her reward you should remind them that when the timer goes off, he/she should stop using it. Then check with them to see if they heard you or if they understand You can provide a verbal prompt, "What will happen when the timer goes off?" If they cannot answer but they are normally verbal, then supply the sentence starter, "When the timer goes off, I stop…" If the student has limited vocabulary, spell out timer on his/her device, or on paper or white board. If the student has a vocabulary picture system, then search for the picture of the timer, and have him/her press it.

If a student does not agree, present a different reward, or simply have the student pick out the reward (in symbol/picture form) of his/her choosing. You may want to alter the language, and present fewer words for him/her to understand with wait time (Start with 1-2 minutes.) Repeat his/her choices whilst pointing to visuals. If they are too frustrated, move onto a new activity (perhaps a sensory break), then give wait time before you present the choices again.

If the student has finally agreed and is currently working for the reward, set a timer for BOTH the work and the reward activity, especially if it is not a preferred activity. A reward should not be given indefinitely because it will hinder the next activity. Set down the timer in front of the child, and before the timer runs out, remind him/ her about the timer running out and what he/she is expected to do. When the timer runs out, show the timer to the child, pause, "E.g. The timer ran out, __ Name __ you did a great job writing your name. Now we are going to stop and move on to

____." Here you may want to show what is next in the student's visual schedule. Then repeat the "First—Then" chart. Students with autism can sometimes be easily distracted, and even though you are speaking, he/she may not have heard you. It's okay to help them by providing a physical prompt, slowly, while repeating, "The timer ran out so let's stop using the computer." If the child has a device, use the device to tap out what you are saying such as "timer stopped" or "finished." If the student did not realize the timer went off, then show it to them. Then, direct to what comes next on the visual schedule. You can provide a visual that shows calm hands, or a stop sign. Repeat the "First—Then" chart as needed to help the student go about their day or when needed upon facing a non-preferred/ challenging activity. Reassure the student that he/she can work for the computer again.

Single Visual

If a student cannot yet focus on the "First-Then" chart, use a single visual instead of the next activity. For example, if you are going to transition to a special activity such as physical education, music, art, or library, then use a single visual of a symbol that represents that activity. You can also use realistic photos of the teachers themselves and even stick it on a representational object. For example, pair a paintbrush and attach a photo of the art teacher to it. As the student is about to transition, show them the photo and have them hold it. You can have the student walk with this object, or give it to the art teacher as part of checking in. Using single visuals is more concrete, and helps the student to focus on one-step directives before graduating to using double visuals.

Sticker Chart

You can use a sticker chart with all the students' names. The students can earn stickers throughout the day and place the stickers next to their name. Students like to see their rewards, a sticker chart is a great way for them to see the progress they have made. I can find tons of sticks, charts, posterboard, etc. at my local dollar store. Additionally, if you are computer savvy, or if someone you know is then you can make it on a word processing program, print appropriate pictures, then laminate, and use Velcro dots to attach them to a posterboard for repeated use.

With sticker charts, it's best to use your judgment on whether a child should receive a reward after a certain number of stickers. When he/she earns three stickers, five stickers, etc., perhaps you want the child to earn rewards with each sticker they earn such as pencil, eraser or even a larger, fancier sticker to take home or wear. If you don't want to spend money, students can work for fun activities in the classroom such as coloring time, computer time, etc. If you are using a sticker chart, you can place a new sticker to show that they completed the activity and received a reward. At the end of the day, depending on the sticker chart, the student can see all the stickers he/she worked for.

Think about how many stickers can be earned, and for what duration. For example, you may have three stickers per thirty-fifty-minute intervals. One sticker is for sitting, another sticker is for calm hands/ hands to self, and the third is for completing an activity. If John was sitting with calm hands, then he would get two or three stickers. Try giving him a sticker for simply writing his name on his work or perhaps, after completing one side of his work will earn him another sticker. Of course, if John is not motivated by stickers, then this would not be the correct rewards system. John wants to be rewarded for his work, especially if it is a nonpreferred activity. At the workplace, we are rewarded for our work with money and perhaps benefits.

What Am I Working For? Chart

The "What am I working for?" chart is much like the "First-Then" chart. You can find them through a web search and can even create your own. The difference between the "First-Then" and "What am I working for?" board is that one shows the work activity, and the other does not. If a student is in the middle of working and decides to break a rule such as hitting another student, point to the "Hands To Myself" while the student is working, to remind the student what he/she is working toward and what they must do. You can also circle it with a dry/erase marker or draw an arrow pointing to that picture.

Another "I Am Working For" chart provided small pictures of rewards like pictures of trophies, ribbons, cartoons to show the student the good work he/she put in for that day. It is a collection of the rewards they received. The chart is attached to the top of a small bin that would be typically used for pencils, crayons, etc. Inside the bin, put all the Velcro symbols including the trophies, for easy access. So, essentially it becomes a behavioral management mini-kit.

When do you give the first trophy?

The first trophy should be given in the first period or the beginning of the day. If the student got a trophy, he/she can take out this picture and Velcro it on the chart on the left side, then the next trophy would be attached on the right side of the first, and so on. So, by the end of the day when all the trophies cover up the chart, the student can see his/her achievement for the day.

Points Systems

A points system is determined by how many points you want to give or take away. A coworker of mine used a 10-point system. She relayed to me that she's had success with this system after trial and error with other token economy systems, including the positive behavior intervention support program we were told to use that was essentially a communication app that was linked to the school community. It seemed to have worked for her. She had students with autism, Oppositional Defiance Disorder who were also labeled as emotionally disturbed.

The way the system works is, each student starts off with ten points. If they are not following the classroom/ school rules, for example, keeping their hands to themselves, or following instructions, given differentiation and breaks, then they will lose a point. However, they can always make up a point after losing. From their observations, this system has worked for them. Students were able to learn more effectively.

A rule of thumb for any token economy/ reward system is you have to MAKE the student interested. You have to come across as someone who feels the rewards system is very important. When you give a point then make it a big deal! Think of it almost like acting if it is otherwise difficult for you to get into that frame of mind. You are playing the part as Mr./Miss/Ms./Mrs. So And So who strongly believes in this point system, and you are interested in seeing who gets a point next. Think of it like a gameshow and you're the host or, you are in the middle of the Super Bowl and are taking a bet on which team wins and loses—you watch the game then suddenly, SCORE! Another point goes to the Red Team! I am not saying you have to yell and scream, but you get the picture. Try your best to be excited because only you can make them care about it. If you are not interested and/or bored by it, then chances are they will feel the same.

Let's say, there are four different points to be given within a certain time frame, let's say per 50-minute academic period. In other words, a student can get up to four points during that time. For example, Jane can get <u>one point</u> for looking and listening, another point for being safe (meaning sitting with her feet on the ground and keeping her hands to herself), and a third point for doing her work. A fourth point could be a specific goal you make such as "Asking for help when needed, raising hand to speak, waiting her turn, etc." You can be creative and decide what goal you would like to work on with your student. Give rewards that you know students like as a whole group. Remind students of body awareness and call them out for positive reinforcement.

"I like the way Johnny is sitting with his back against the chair, and feet on the floor. He's getting a point." This also gives them positive attention. Keep in mind, all students will sometimes break/ bend rules or "test you" for negative attention. They don't see attention as good or bad, they simply see it as attention. When this happens, use your best judgement as to how to proceed with students who seek negative attention. Catch them when they are doing something good, no matter how small.

"Great job holding the door John. You are very kind to your friends."

"Thank you for passing out the pencils. You are very helpful."

Give positive praise in moments when students are going about their day to make them aware that they are behaving in a positive manner. Conduct your classroom day, making yourself aware to these positive actions. Give verbal praise, points, and show visuals of "Great Job." Give positive attention and carry out your behavior intervention strategies. Reward students appropriately for exhibiting behavior conducive to the learning environment.

Chapter 3: Parent/Teacher Conferences

With parents, I feel like first impressions will set the tone for the rest of the year. I try my best to have open communication; too much is just enough. If you speak to parents weekly or biweekly, then you will run into few, if any, issues. With parental consent, send pictures of their children doing work. Make sure you don't leave any questionable items or things happening around in the background! Scan the picture and all the small details that you assume people would typically ignore. For example, if you have a behavior chart that you use as part of your behavior management, then you accidentally take a picture of John in the Red Zone, parents will immediately ask you, "Why is my child on red?" If you discuss this anyway then it's fine, but if you wanted to discuss something else and only have a certain amount of time, then it is a good idea to take precautions.

What if you take a photo of John doing his work but the Teacher's Aide is on his/her phone. This is a bad look and makes it seem like he/she is not doing their job (including you for allowing this to happen). Perhaps, he/she received an urgent phone call, and there was a valid reason. It is still bound to raise a few eyebrows.

What do you talk about during parent/teacher conferences? In your first few chats with parents, you should ask them what goals they have for their child, academically and socially. Ask parents about student interests and what motivates the student. This information can be useful in driving instruction and heightening student engagement. Reading a student's IEP is good, but you also want to see which goals the parent mentions. Some goals may take more precedence than others, and actually, they may be completely different from the previous IEP.

Perhaps, over the summer, the student has mastered all his/her goals and the parent is helping him/her with more challenging material. Ask how he/she works with the child at home: Is there a way to get John to do his homework? If so, what is it? Perhaps, it's a fidget spinner, and what if you had one in your Supplies Closet? You can take it out and save it in the event John needs a little extra motivation. It's always good to know: what would he be willing to work for?

Adults are motivated by rewards as well. Some are motivated by money more than others. Whether it's a summer vacation, down payment on a new house, etc. we are motivated to put in work. Besides knowing this, also, let the parents know that you are here to support the child. If there are additional supports they need at home like perhaps a morning routine visual schedule, it would be a good idea to assist them in this. It would help your relationship with the parent, and perhaps encourage them to communicate more effectively with you. Perhaps, several parents have this similar challenge; if so, then let it drive your instruction. Let morning routine and hygiene be a focus on your next adaptive/self-care lesson. Go over what to expect and the steps such as wetting the toothbrush, putting on toothpaste, etc. Read books and engage in dramatic play. Keep the lines of discussion open between you and the parents.

Upload pictures of visual supports that you use in the classroom to show parents, and after obtaining parental consent, show pictures of students working. For parents, as well as administrators, take pictures and provide evidence of differentiated instruction. Parents want to see that you are not providing work that is too easy, nor too hard either. When parents understand what you are working on in class and what their child is having trouble with, they are more likely to extend support at home.

Stimming

During parent-teacher conferences, I often get asked, "How do I stop him from clapping?" or " Why does she make noises?" Students with autism can engage in self-stimulating and repetitive behaviors commonly known as "stimming." This is a symptom of autism. According to my observations, my students stim when they are nervous, bored, or excited. It seems like a natural thing for them.

I can be in the middle of a whole group lesson when a student looking in the opposite direction of where I am is clapping and smiling, or flailing their hands toward the ceiling. Stimming is not a "bad" thing; it's a "different" thing. One student with ASD will not stim exactly like the next. Adults in a doctor's office may flip their pens and click excessively or rock their feet. Most of the time, it is a way for us to cope with our current situation. Do not see stimming as a negative thing, and don't try to erase it with medication. If it's a cause for interruption and is loud, then redirect the behavior using verbal and visual strategies. Show the student a visual of a more appropriate action. If the student was clapping or creating noise whilst you were teaching, choose a quieter alternative such as hands resting on the table, stroking, or holding a fidget/ calming down toy. Once the stim has reached a reasonable volume then continue with the lesson. If not, then consider adapting to his/her stim. Perhaps, the instruction is not engaging enough; perhaps they need to get up and be a part of it or are ready for a more challenging hands-on activity. It's always best to be flexible, not only in lesson planning, but also in implementation.

A second strategy is to use foam or durable sheets that provide tactile stimulation and cut out a hand shape and place on the table. When you verbally prompt the student, "Calm hands," then the student will put his/her hands on the table and can touch and rub his/her fingers on the foamy hand cut outs. You can use Velcro dots and attach them to the back of the foam hands to keep them on the table. This has worked, but you have to be watchful. If you allow the child to play with the foam hands, he/she may be so distracted with them that the foam hands end up peeling off the table and the Velcro dots may also be peeled off. The foam hands are not for playing with, it's only to provide a temporary relief with tactile support paired with a verbal and visual prompt. Afterward the student can resume with the activity. They are only to keep the child's hands down in a calm manner.

If the banging persists throughout the activity, then stop and prompt, "Calm hands." You can flash the visual picture or point to the foam hands. Doing this once or twice will not end this behavior. You will need to repeat the prompt as often as needed, consistently and firmly. If you want to target behavior, then implement a token economy system. You may even start a rewards chart with a picture of the calm hands. For every time that the student places his/her hands on the foam cut outs, add a sticker to his/her chart. You can also use verbal praise or do a point system. Verbal praise should be immediate. On each classroom table, I will tape the individualized visuals that each of the students need. I can stick "calm hands" visuals on the table so that when he looks at the table, he'll automatically see a picture of calm hands or the foam cut outs.

Redirect the behavior by transitioning the child into another activity where they can refocus and eliminate excessive stimuli. Stimming could result from being at one place and doing one activity for a longer period. The student may just need to stand up and stretch for five minutes and sit back down. If he/she does not want to return to the activity after the break and is resisting strategies, cut the activity short and return another day.

If you have a token economy system such as a sticker chart, then he/she will not receive a sticker or reward for that activity. If you move onto something different then that should be a separate opportunity for a reward. Increase the time slowly as this will help the student become desensitized to the unpreferred activity as the student gets more comfortable with it. An alternative to this would be extending time; give five-minute breaks per period. Set a timer in front of the student for shorter intervals, then provide the reinforcer. For example, if the student is working for a stuffed animal, then allow the student to touch or pet the stuffed animal for several seconds then take back the reward and continue then stop again in this fashion.

Out in the Community

Whether it is crossing the street to play at a neighborhood park or buying dinner at the supermarket, children need to be taught the behavioral norms and expectations for these places. For example, before you go to the supermarket it's a good idea to make a list of the things you will get at the supermarket. Explain that these are the items you'll be looking for. Do a picture walk (if you can find pictures) or play a video of someone shopping at the supermarket. Point out what they are doing such as walking down the aisle on one side, they are taking only what they need, etc. Go over scenarios, for example, if you are walking and trying to get a certain item, but someone is blocking you because they are also shopping, then you can wait and say, "Excuse me."

At the supermarket, you are expected to wait in line/ wait your turn for the cashier to ring up your food and check you out. Prior to placing your food on the conveyor belt, you can say, "Hello" because that is the polite thing to do. After you finished checking out, what do 'we' do after? How do 'we' safely get to the parking lot? Extend this lesson as you see fit, read social stories, show visuals, act out scenarios, and practice these living skills. Go over social stories and use dramatic play to act out scenarios. Use a communication board to review things that you will say such as, "Excuse me."

Focus on real-world examples, and think about the goal. Is the goal to promote safety? Is it to help the student assimilate into the community in more socially acceptable ways? Perhaps, all the above. Don't forget to break down the lesson into smaller parts. You don't have to get through everything in one day. For example, when discussing how to cross the street, teach what crosswalks and traffic lights mean, and the rules of the sidewalk and street. Teach about the community to integrate kids into daily life. It takes practice because you are practicing multiple skills while communicating with others.

Develop a unit for the month, for example, for three weeks work on hygiene: learning how to brush teeth, shampoo hair, and wash hands and face. Spend the last week of the month reviewing, then move on to a new topic next month. When navigating different settings with your child, I would recommend using verbal with visual prompts first for the expectations that you want him/her to follow. Keep on hand visuals that you can refer to before and during an activity. For example, if the activity is walking the dog, upon exiting your home, prompt the child on expected behavior. You can decide what that will be. Perhaps, you may want to remind them "Do not run- Danger" or "Walking Feet," you can say "Hold hands" if it is age appropriate, complete with pictures and accompanying text. Take pictures of the streets you'll be walking on, point out traffic lights/ crosswalks, and for additional prompts you can hold "STOP" and "GO" visuals.

Chapter 4: The Classroom Environment

In a classroom setting, I often rotate students' seats based on their academic and social needs. I try to eliminate potential distractions that may impede their learning. Students come from all kinds of backgrounds, culture, and religion. There may be children suffering from previous trauma in their lives and events can trigger them and remind them of a terrifying situation. They can suffer from PTSD and not know how to express it. We may never know exactly what traumas they face, and sometimes we have to really observe their behaviors, and read signs.

In my experience, it becomes trial and error. You need to get to know your students/children to find their triggers if any during learning time, mealtime, etc. I assign seats in a way that will be conducive to the learning environment. I have had a nonverbal student who was afraid of a cartoon character on another peer's shirt/bookbag. Take note, make observations, and continue to speak with parents. During lunchtime, you don't simply leave students to eat if you're on lunch duty. You must watch their behaviors and make sure everyone is supported and no one is ignored. A student may not be able to explain what he/she needs. In this case, if a student does not already have a speech/ communication device, support them with communication boards. Prompt the student with a verbal question, "What do you need?" Hold up the board. The student can point to "fork, spoon, open, etc." You can also ask, "Do you need a fork?" Then the student can say or point to yes, or no.

In the beginning, start with fewer symbols, then gradually work up to exposing him/her to more vocabulary words with pictures and text. It is important to be mindful of the student's needs, behavioral triggers, and skill set. In class, if John has difficulty seeing the board, place him closer to it so that he can see. If Jane is easily distracted, place her in an area with the least possible distractions. If John runs to get water every five minutes and it is causing him to miss out on most of the lesson, and its distracting other kids then place him farthest away from the water fountain. If Jane touches and takes out math manipulatives to play during whole group instruction, despite several verbal prompts from her teacher, then seat her closer to the board and farther away from the math manipulatives.

It takes trial and error as well as observations to find out where you should place students and what would help them learn best. In the beginning of the year, teach students how to express their emotions. Teach them how to illustrate their mood using pictures and symbols. Help them to reflect and provide vocabulary to help express and recognize their emotions. Think aloud to model the thinking process, after posing the question, "I feel happy today because..."

Facilitate Language for Peer Communication

I had a student who constantly kept touching another student. The student was not physically harmful. He was playful, but the other student did not understand what he was trying to accomplish. He had difficulty speaking and could only make very few and selected utterances provided with multiple prompts and repetitions. This student seemed to want to make friends but didn't know how.

Model appropriate conversation with the use of visual and verbal cues. Use a communication board that doubles as a vocabulary word bank. Point to "Hello" then "How are you?" Help facilitate communication with peers. You need to model how this looks and facilitate examples of appropriate play and conversation. I would facilitate language and explain to the other student, "John wants to say hello. Say, "Good morning, Jane. Can John shake your hand?" I've taught my students how to shake hands while looking each other in the eyes when they greet one another. If the student wants to say, 'Hi' but does not want to shake hands, then try again next time. Once in a while, some will change their mind, while others will need alternatives, or more modeling and positive reinforcement.

Give them an opportunity to reflect on their emotions and share with their peers during your morning meeting/ circle time. You can have them practice asking, "How was your day? How do you feel?" Model this exchange with another adult before you have students do it. Provide a visual where they can point as a reply to their peer if they are having difficulty speaking. Make this a part of the routine and have them practice it with different people in and out of the classroom. Look for opportunities for communication. I did this during the morning routine, and by the end of the year, the students no longer needed me to help prompt them to ask their peer, "How was your day?" or "How do you feel?" They knew the routine.

Focus on What Students CAN Do

If a student asks another student "Can you share your snack?" that is for the student to say, "Yes" or "No." It's not for you to decide or control unless the other student that is asking has allergies. Then, you will say, "No. He cannot share his snack." The student with the snack can say no, and that is a valid answer. Imagine how defeated a child could feel if his/her aid/teacher answered, "Yes" to "Can I have your snack? Or can I borrow your scissors?" and the aid/teacher went ahead, reached into the child's desk or food tray, and gave it away. Give students an opportunity to show what they can do, to respond how they want, and to express themselves. "No" is an answer too. Help students to answer yes/no and share their opinions by providing sentence starters and word banks.

Nonverbal students can use an AAC (Augmentative and Alternative Communication) device and have them select Yes/ or No or have them use gestures. Focus on what students CAN do – not what they can't do. Students with autism very often have other disabilities and this can affect their speech and fine motor coordination. Even so, taught helplessness is never good. In my experience with a student, one of his goals was to take off /put on his jacket. He had difficulty with the morning routine and often did not stand up for exercise. Toward the end of the year, he was able to take off/ hang up/ put on his coat along with his bookbag, take out his lunchbox, and open his lunchbox himself. He laughed and smiled so happily during movement breaks. Students with autism need that same stern approach as students in general education. They do NOT need learned helplessness. Start with one step at a time to help them to be self-directed, independent, and empowered.

Immediate Visual Praise

If there is a behavior that you'd like to address that is embedded within steps of a daily routine, creating visuals of the step by step even such as "brushing teeth, morning routine, transitioning from house to bus, etc." Each step can be followed with "Good Job" symbol on a communication board. If he/she does not complete a step then do not provide praise—go to the next one after sufficient wait time, physical prompting, hand over hands. If they complete a step, they should still get the verbal praise for that step regardless if they didn't finish the previous one. The point is to give positive praise, and to give immediate feedback.

As small as these steps may seem, they are still opportunities for praise. When students follow these steps, they will get used to, "Good Job" after they follow a direction. Verbal praise is given after they follow a direction, so if they do not hear, "Good Job," they may say it themselves. Students may put effort into what is asked so they could obtain that immediate praise ,"Good Job." Try to be specific with praises so students know what part exactly was "good;" opt for "Good job in writing your name," "Great asking," "Good job in sitting calmly."

Verbal praise is a great reward, but in the beginning, children may need more concrete and tangible rewards such as a sticker, a toy, a favorite snack, etc. However, the goal that we recommend is to slowly ween off these rewards and aim toward positive and verbal praise.

Spend 1:1 Time With Students Individually

Make it a point to spend time playing with the child/student during

choice time. Do things together that they find fun. Create time to bond and build a relationship with them. Be silly, empathize, and talk to them. Spending time with students helps foster trust, thus creating perfect groundwork for teaching. If students trust and like you then they are more willing to listen to you. They understand that with you they can have fun and learn. Continue to spend time with students and give them 1:1 attention. In fact, in the beginning of the year, work on building this relationship. Focus on creating a safe environment conducive to learning.

Students can compete with their peers for your attention and may try to obtain it in different ways. Sometimes, students may be "attention seekers." This means they will purposely act in a way where you will immediately stop and give them your full attention. Reinforcing behavior that is not ideal for the classroom environment is the same as providing negative attention. Sometimes, negative attention supersedes positive attention because we put more effort into it. Be sure that you give students more verbal praise when they are illustrating positive behaviors than negative. One should outweigh the other. Give more attention to when he/she does something right than wrong. Always give children the opportunity to self-correct because in some cases, students may just need sufficient wait time. Then, when he/she is acting with the desired behavior, make a big deal out of it! Alert them to the fact that they are succeeding, for example, "*Wow*, John. You are sitting *so* nicely, and I really like how you are keeping your hands to yourself. You're being such a good friend!" This can be followed with a point, or sticker, depending on your token economy system, after the task/ activity is completed.

Narrating your thinking process as you model desired behavior can help students plan step-by-step. Give them jobs to make this happen. Some jobs can be turning the lights on or off, passing out the pencils, or collecting notebooks. Give them a sense of empowerment in other aspects in the classroom environment. Find a way to give responsibility to students by giving classroom jobs. Use prompting as needed and modify when appropriate. Use supportive staff as human resources that can help as well.

Too Much Noise!

Students with autism tend to be overly stimulated or under stimulated. Hypersensitive students are more sensitive to sounds, smells and visual stimuli more than students that do not have autism. Sounds may hurt them, and this may make them bite, scream, put their hands on their ears, or elope. For students who are hypersensitive, use noise canceling or reducing headphones and preferential seating, or place student in areas with less noise to alleviate some of the stress.

I had one student who would constantly bump into things and grab his ears. It wasn't until I began giving him these thick blue headphones that he appeared to be more comfortable whilst sitting in his chair. It was my suspicion that feedback from loud noises caused him to be off-balance while he walked, which was not safe for him. The use of noise reduction headphones can be an accommodation added to a student's IEP. It can also be useful in areas with high volumes of noise such as a movie theater, theme park, and playground, to name a few.

Stephanie L. Lindner

Chapter 5: Meltdowns

In handling meltdowns, I try to focus on preventative measures and teach students techniques to self-regulate. For students to carry strategies into multiple settings, it's important to first gather as much data as you can. You can do this by reaching out to staff who had him/her the previous year such as Occupational Therapists, Speech and Language Pathologists, Physical Therapists, teachers, and paraprofessionals. Doing this will give you a better understanding of the child and you will be more prepared upon meeting him/her. It can give you insights to potential triggers, life at home, interests, etc.

A student can be "set off" during transitions, certain triggers which are varied by situation. Even certain people and other students can be triggers. These triggers may be connected to an event that happened in the past from a certain traumatic experience. As teachers, we will have no idea what these traumatic experiences are and may never find out. We may have an inclination on the situation at home but if we don't get information from the parent or staff member, then we are essentially left in the dark. It's important to be mindful of this.

Learning about your student will help prevent you making unnecessary assumptions about his/her behavior. If a student is diagnosed with "emotionally disturbed" or "oppositional defiance disorder" it means we must do everything in our power to create the safest and most nurturing environment for the child. If the student is going through a similar situation or cannot seem to move past a certain event, then they may script or retell the event word for word. The student will be replaying an event, although he/she can be in a different environment.

Scripting is a sign of frustration, and it is an event the child is trying to understand. For me, it is an indicator that they are experiencing frustration of some kind. Neurotypical adults tend to go over scenarios and feel the same frustration as they did before. Perhaps, we wonder: what could we have done differently if a meltdown were to occur? Why did he/she say or do that? We can obsess over things that happened to us in the past. Perhaps, at the time we didn't come up with the right words to say to defend and protect ourselves. Perhaps, we are still confused and hurt over the incident.

When students display aggression from a meltdown, there can be many causes. As teachers, we are also therapists and *confidantes*. This is why it is so important to know your students, not just their disability, but as people who are a part of our community.

Throughout the school year, teachers are learning from their students as well. We learn their interests, areas of need, areas of strength, and what triggers them. Again, triggers can be situations, actions, or people that remind someone of a stressful event. Taking data on instances of meltdowns when they occur will help you monitor a student's progress or regression with a certain reinforcer. In this way, we can deal with meltdowns through prevention, through conferences with parents, positive reinforcement, redirection, and verbal, visual, and physical prompts.

There may be certain behaviors that you can target, one at a time. If a student has several meltdowns throughout the day, without a behavior plan then it is important to take anecdotes for each event, writing the date, time, how long it lasted, what happened before (what triggered the behavior) and if there was something to deescalate the behavior. If meltdowns happen several times every day for six weeks or more, then take your anecdotes and refer them to the school counselor. After determining a plan of action together, implement it.

Let's discuss a few preventative strategies. The following are not the only strategies there are when dealing with meltdowns. Most of these strategies I have tried and others I have seen work in my experience from colleagues. One intervention may work for one student but not the other. I can only tell you what has worked based on my observations.

In the beginning of the year, I focus on positive behavior support, and social-emotional learning. We learn about being a friend, making choices and following classroom safety rules. Why do I make it a point to do this? I do this to make boundaries and expectations clear; it helps set the tone for a positive learning environment. In addition, students learn to self-reflect and express themselves in multiple ways. We engage in this learning for several months before deep diving into academics. Take the time and plan to emphasize what it means to be in your classroom. Engage in different calm down activities because what may work for one child may not work for the other.

If you have a hard first few weeks, don't beat yourself up. You are trying the best that you can, and a positive and organized routine and structure does not happen overnight. Your child wants consistency. As a parent, you have the power to set the tone and support your child in different aspects. Allow the child for opportunities of control; allow for independence and confidence. You are with the child more than the teacher, and you have more years of experience and more detailed background knowledge. In working together, both parents and teachers may learn new strategies to support students in and out of school.

Additionally, in handling meltdowns in the classroom you must be in the right frame of mind, because this takes a whole lot of patience, persistence, and informed decision making. So, set aside time daily for self-care to balance out your work life and personal life as well. Teachers often bring homework wherever they go; they don't leave it at the door to their classroom and go about their day. There is always work to be done and without adequate prep and collaborative time, a large amount of paperwork will pile up at your desk.

My ex-coworker used to bring her work to the hair

salon and grade papers while she was getting her hair highlighted at the salon. I'm sure this seems efficient, but I would advise not to do work during moments of self-care. You need that time for yourself; you are equally important. In not providing any self-care, you may be agitated, on edge, and feel overworked. You need time daily to self-reflect and provide calm to your routine. It is important and it is worth your time.

To process the day or week, recharging your batteries and centering yourself requires that you give yourself a break, whether you take a moment in your day to simply be calm, focus on breathing techniques, and being present and still. As a teacher, you will also teach self-care and meditative techniques to your students. As you create a consistent routine for your students, create a consistent routine for yourself. As you provide sensory breaks for your students, provide self-care breaks for yourself. Coming to work in a negative frame of mind doesn't make you a bad person. You just have to decide if you want to keep that frame of mind, and take action to also be good to yourself so that you can be your best self.

Calm Down Area

In a situation, where it's important to deescalate a child's behavior due to the fact that they are displaying violent behavior to themselves or others, it is important to place them in a designated

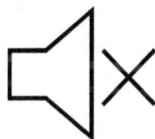

calm down area where they can see visuals with steps to calm down. They need to know where this calm down or quiet area is. They need to know that they have access to go there when they want to. In the calm down corner, there should be one chair beside a wall facing the class. They are essentially temporarily taking a break from that activity from the farthest part of the room. In the calm down space, there may be cardboard pieces with different textures that they can touch, some with a mixture of sparkly, and translucent beads, while others are covered in dry rice/ beans, etc. There may also be soft fabrics and rough fabrics in small squares against the wall.

When they are sent to the calm down area, it is because they are showing signs of frustration that is not on par with the behavior expectations of the school community. At this time, they need to be redirected. Reinforce the behavior management strategies (What am I working for? First—Then, etc.) Afterward, monitor the child's breathing as it may indicate they are calming down. In this case, continue steps for calming down. These steps can include taking deep breaths, "Let's take ten deep breaths. The first five we'll do together." After taking deep breaths, I suggest another step like counting back from ten so that the child is returned to a calm and steady pace. Then, remind them of the reinforcer, "What are you working for?" Show visuals, or have the child use his/her tablet. Redirect with verbal/ visual cues and move to a different activity as you slowly work to desensitize them to the unpreferred activity.

For instance, instead of biting an adult or another peer, perhaps they may squeeze a beanbag, rip up/ cut up paper, touch the sensory wall, etc. Targeting the behavior and teaching "Hands down" or saying "Stop" may not work for all students. They need a replacement.

Students with autism enjoy routine and feel safe with it. If you were away and someone else was with your child, by routine they may script the calm down technique when they are in the calm down corner to self soothe and stick to their routine.

In addition, when you are saying the cue, say it in the same tone as you normally speak. In the situation, where the child will constantly touch another child and disregard "Calm Hands," remove one of the children and place him/her in a different seat. Be strategic where the child is placed in the situation that he/she is in. Provide visual cues, picture reminders that show the accepted expectation. If a child cannot keep his/her hands off something provide a visual cue that shows hands that are folded. You can point to remind the child silently or give a verbal and visual cue. If the child does not listen to a visual, verbal or both then resort to the physical prompt, and accommodate the surroundings for that child. If a student walks to the calm down corner, and cries or screams louder immediately jump into your calm down routine. Show an analog timer of 30 seconds or so of their calm down time left. Redirect their focus to the timer. You can set it down where they can see it. Do not give it to them if you feel that they will throw it. Placing sensory boards against the wall in the area. The kids like to touch and feel these. You can redirect their focus to prevent the Meltdown from escalating. You can pair items like weighted vest, or vibrating tools to help the student as well.

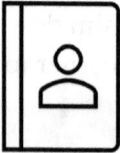

Decreasing Visual Stimuli With a Poster Board

Some students may need a calm, simple area where they can decompress. Decreasing excessive stimuli in the environment (for example closing the window, lowering the blinds) can help with this, even as a preventative measure. Use a plain white foldable cardboard/ poster board to block excessive stimuli. I had a student who would cry when others looked at him, and he would also constantly touch things and get out of his chair to inspect things about the classroom. I started putting a white poster board in front of him so that way he would be more focused on the lesson than a student looking at him, drawing any sort of negative attention. Once I saw that it was helping, I would use it less and less and only when needed. This helped him stay in his area and pay less attention to other students.

At home, you can use the white poster board to fold around the table to complete an activity so he/she is not distracted by a sibling or pet. You can use your discretion on what activity you would like to focus on with your child. Keep it in an area that is easily accessible to you. I kept mine behind one of my library shelves. I simply would take it out, fold it into three parts, and place it on his desk. The best thing about this was that I was able to pick it up and reuse it for another student. It's cheap, simple, and effective. At home, when students are at the table trying to complete homework, a fun activity or simply to finish eating a meal, this can help them block out excessive stimuli. It is recommended to be used on and off when necessary for only several minutes at a time.

Biting

In my experience, students who are prone to biting are frustrated for reasons that we can try to understand. Sometimes, there is a restlessness due to a chemical imbalance that betrays the body. John will usually try to escape from an activity, run about the room, or fall out of his chair. But he usually enjoys sensory play where he can have touchable materials that he can easily operate.

I have observed a student taking someone else's hand to place under their chin to rub back and forth, as to create some form of compression and stimulation if I were to guess. Biting can be due to frustration for not being able to use words and being able to communicate wants and needs (*see* Maslow's Hierarchy of Needs). Create a communication board with basic needs like "water, toilet, food, etc." Pointing to a basic need that is not being met can alleviate stress and hence prevent a meltdown. You have to model how to use the board and teach the student to use each symbol functionally. For example, during snack time while all the students are sitting in their seats around the table having their snack, John still has his snack in front of him, but he needs help opening his snack. Prompt him to say or point to "open" by placing the symbol next to him, point and verbalize the word if he is showing you which snack he wants. It's important that you give John ample wait time before opening his snack, even if he is a little impatient. Continue this method as often as you see John during snack time until he internalizes it and can functionally point or say open in multiple settings.

Biting that seems unprovoked can happen during transition times because of distractors and engaging in nonpreferred activities. Give these students a transition tool they can use during transitions only—whether it's a sensory toy, a snack, or a tablet to prevent the behavior from happening. Include sensory opportunities that is fun throughout the day for the student to engage in. Do not focus solely on academic work, especially if this is the reason why the student is escaping. Integrate academics *slowly* through creative means and play, so it does not feel like work.

If you want to focus solely on academics without any other forms of sensory opportunities, then you won't get much work done with a student who is trying to bite in order to escape. Make students WANT to be there. Make learning fun, and if mostly play-based in early childhood, provide necessary prompts for age-appropriate learning opportunities. Continue to reinforce boundaries and rules with visual prompts, implement therapeutic tools and sensory diet, for example, weighted vest or sensory brushes. Continue with your token economy system that is in place.

> Reflect on what happens before he/she bites.
> Can he/she communicate his/her wants and needs?
> What will he/she get after biting?
> What will be the consequence?
> Will the consequence be the same every time?

Perhaps, the consequence is providing calm-down strategies and walking the student over to the calm down corner or quiet room. Use calm-down strategies, give them a break if they can follow initial steps in calming down first, decrease stimuli, and transition back. Provide social stories on biting; use real pictures and cartoons also. Make a visual and show the students while they are engaged in that behavior. Students may not understand that there are social norms of behavior in EVERY place they go. They may think, I cannot go in the closet and take-out toys at school, but I can do it in my room. I can run in the playground, but not in the street. If they are taught what is appropriate behavior and are taught negative behavior carries consequences with it in their class, but not elsewhere that's when things can get very confusing. It's important to carry over and scaffold what a student has learned whilst adding more lessons in social behavior.

Autism can often be referred to as a "social disorder." The child may lack the social skills for another child of their age and these skills may take longer to build. No matter what end of the spectrum the student is on, communicate boundaries in every place they go. In my experience, I would often see the children who bit or slapped other kids be taken into a quieter area that was separate from their classroom. Sometimes, students can be sent to a quiet area in the classroom to calm down, reflect and that can work if it will only take the student several minutes. Students who are hypersensitive to noise and can engage in meltdowns which can cause a chain reaction that triggers several more students. Then suddenly, all students are screaming and upset in the room and feel uncomfortable.

Students need consistency, organization, and they need to understand what their boundaries are and why they have them in every place they go. The boundaries must be reviewed before the student transitions to the next place and reminders should be given when needed. Parents and teachers need to be on the same page not in different books altogether if you get my drift.

Your Tone of Voice Says a Lot

Depending on the student, talking in a loud and assertive tone can also help students break out of their meltdown mode. However, I've seen students who do not respond to this tone and will respond more positively to calm and sincere, yet stern instead. Teachers and parents do not have never-ending abundance of patience. Sometimes, situations require us to take a few breaths ourselves, regroup, and reassess. Reflect on yourself. *When you are upset—which tone reaches you more: the assertive one or the calm and understanding tone?* When the student seems to be spiraling, try to find ways to give them a little control. Give students a choice, even when they are upset.

Even when students are challenging me and testing me, I try my best to speak clearly, assertively, and calmly. It is not a bubbly, friendly voice. It is a calm—assertive one. Remember, do not show them that you are mad. Try to always provide opportunities for positive reinforcement.

Also, remember that it is normal to feel frustrated, whether its during teaching or parenting, because we are all human. Perhaps, you only got four hours of sleep last night and John is screaming, crying, and biting. You must do your best to help John understand what he needs to do at that very moment to get back on track. Detach yourself and jump into your routine to deescalate the situation. Sometimes, when students are in the middle of a full-blown meltdown—they just need time to let it out. It is a power struggle. They want to be heard. Before taking them out of the room, try to go to the calming area of the classroom, or if you are at home –the room you are in at the time.

Teachers do not like to restrain children or touch them at all because most of the time we are not trained in these methods. If you are, then you can safely and accurately provide the restraints if you feel it is necessary for the child. Validate a students' emotions and show them how you sympathize and can relate to them. When we are frustrated or hurt, we may call up one of our parents, a best friend, or significant other. We need to hear their support, their comfort. We need the opportunity to express ourselves.

Oftentimes, WE as adults have difficulty expressing ourselves. We can be frustrated from several things and finally—we blow up, and can lash out against those that are close to us. Sometimes, WE need to relax or work out the frustration. We have the power to do things to make us feel better, although we do not always do them. Sometimes, WE ignore calm down techniques and we let our emotions take control. We sometimes feel better expressing ourselves, talking it out with someone, or doing something that relaxes us and makes us happy. We Meltdown because we are not getting what we want, or we are frustrated by the action of another.

It is important to not give in and give up on your

child and what you want your child to do that is best for him/her. Perhaps, you want him/her to become a better reader, or be able to add numbers. Academic and life skills take time, and as a parent and teacher, it is important to want those things for your child. Students with autism need structure as we all do. They need balance and need rewards, too. Have you ever rewarded yourself? Maybe you bought yourself something nice and think, *It is ok to buy this because I worked hard for it all week.* You tell yourself, *I worked hard all year and I was the best I could be so I will reward myself.* It feels good. Maybe the rewards are in the form of verbal praise from your boss. It makes you want to continue to work hard and receive another reward. Sometimes, you must tell yourself you did a great job. Students need to recognize they are doing a great job and never miss an opportunity for positive reinforcement.

Adults can choose to react or not to react. It is your choice to act out in the way that you do. We are more aware of what makes us tick and what calms and relaxes us. Students with disabilities and children in general need to be taught strategies for self-regulation; they need this to be modeled.

Let your data guide your instruction. Create a lesson plan and provide a social story of John's trigger, and talk about it with the student. Make these triggers into lessons. If John bites during transitions, spend time on teaching transitions, practice them, watch videos, read books, act it out using puppets. With planning, preparation, and ongoing communication you'll be able to manage meltdowns more thoughtfully.

Transitional Items

If a student is having meltdown, due to transitioning to the next activity, plant transitional items along their path to where they need to go or have them take the item with them as they are walking to the next activity. For example, if a student is transitioning into the classroom, plant small items for every step. If the student likes to play with toy cars, plant a car by the coat area, then if they have to wash their hands to join the class, plant another car by the sink to have him/her collect it as he/she is completing the next step. Then, if the last thing is to sit in a chair by the table, plant the third car on the table. If you want to use one specific item as the transitional toy, try to use that toy only for transitions to maintain the student's interest. After they complete the transition into the next activity, you can decide to remove the item when they are engaged with something else.

Chapter 6: Speech and Language

Students can get very frustrated if they are mad at something but cannot supply the language to express it. Imagine experiencing something you dislike, need, or want and not being able to speak your mind, and not being able to express yourself through any means. What can you use? You can use your body. You can use your emotions. What sounds can you make? You can have a meltdown to express your anger and sadness. You can cry to illustrate your disapproval. These emotions come naturally for us and it can be very frustrating for you if nobody understands you.

I believe that in the case with students who have limited vocabulary and are nonverbal, being taught how to speak or express themselves will dramatically decrease their meltdowns and frustration. Students can learn to express themselves by verbal means, pointing, signing via American Sign Language, and selecting words on their augmentative speech device.

If the student is unhappy but able to communicate, you can use a communication board to ask students why they are sad or mad. They can point to each word "I" "Am" "Sad" "Because" then they can choose from a list of symbols or letters. Proper exposure to vocabulary and opportunities for literacy can aid in sentence structure. A communication board is useful in early childhood because it doubles as a vocabulary word bank. It can have a number of choices like "I am sad because…I am hungry. I am sad because…I did not get the toy I wanted. I am sad because …I miss my family, etc." Have comforting toys or pictures of the students' families in the classroom. Show it to them and this may bring them some comfort. If you know the student has prior knowledge and exposure to vocabulary, provide the sentence starter on his/her tablet and have him/her finish the sentence.

Keep in mind, there are other outside circumstances that may be causing a meltdown. One year, there was a girl in the classroom across from mine. She could not speak but she would often throw herself on the floor and start screaming and crying and she would bite anyone who went close to her. Every day she bit someone. My class shared the same lunch and recess time with her. Once she started learning to use the bathroom on her own—she no longer had to wear a diaper. As a result, the meltdowns decreased exponentially, and she made tremendous progress! Perhaps, certain items of clothing are uncomfortable. Who would want to stay in a wet/ soiled pamper?

Augmentative and Alternative Speech Devices

Students using AAC devices should be encouraged to use their device throughout the course of their day. AAC devices are given if a student needs speech support. There is a process in obtaining one and sometimes it can take years.

Getting a device depends on availability, letters of consent for evaluations, and an interview where the student will be observed in different situations. Some questions to consider are: Does the student need the device to communicate/ express his/her needs? What is the primary form of communication?

If the student is pushing away the device and communicating verbally then he/she may not be recommended for it. If the student shows frustration when answering questions and can barely utter 1-2 words, then there is more of a chance he/she will obtain one. Something to keep in mind: the device is not only used in class with the teacher. In fact, once you have the device as a parent, it becomes your responsibility to make sure he/she is using the device in multiple settings. So, you will learn to use it as well.

If the speech therapist does not provide a manual to the parent on how to use the AAC device, I make a copy of what I have and send it home. The device is useful for many reasons. Sometimes, students can speak but when the time comes to answer a question, they are unable to do so. Here is where the word bank comes in.

When students are asked a question, they have multiple options to choose from; they can engage more in dialogue. Additionally, it also gives a letter bank where they can spell out their answer instead. Students can properly create sentences with meaning after they are exposed to vocabulary.

If a student hasn't had water yet during the day, he/she can use the device to make 1–5-word sentence/request such as "Water" or "Water, please. I want water," or "Can I have water, please?" depending on his/her communication goals and capabilities. If you start in short sentences, aim for more complex sentences as a long-term goal. An adult should help facilitate communication with the AAC device with activities that are appropriate with the time of day.

Communication with non-verbal or low functioning students should be facilitated even during breakfast and lunch. For example, if a student who is practicing answering "Yes" or "No" can be prompted with a question using the device. An example would be, "Do you want water?" After given wait time, if a student does not respond, he/she can be prompted again, with also a physical prompt pointing while saying "Yes" or "No." You can add sign language in addition to the device while giving appropriate wait time.

What are the student's goals? Are they academic? Are they social? Are they behavioral? What do you wish to accomplish? Understand how to add and delete buttons on the device but discuss this first with the speech therapist. If a student is exhibiting a behavior such as taking things from another student, program a button that says "Give" or "Give back." When the student exhibits this behavior, guide the student to the Give Back button, then help him/her give the item back.

Questioning techniques should start with simple

questions, if appropriate, then gradually increase. I have started with two words "Want __?" Students can answer "Yes" or "No." Keep in mind that not all yes and no questions are easy; some require deep thinking and revaluation of one's feelings. Breakfast, lunch, or dinner time can be a great opportunity for speech. Help your child practice answering yes or no questions with every chicken nugget they want, and you can also supply a command.

"Want nuggets?" you ask, and then if you have an AAC device type "Want nuggets?"

Have the student sign, or press "Yes," and say "Yes" if they can speak. Repeat for several times and document how many utterances, what prompts you used, etc. It is important to log information so you can track progress and see what worked and didn't work.

When practicing responses to questions, provide the sentence starter. Provide hand gestures and signs as you are speaking as part of a daily ritual. This way when ask a question, you can provide a physical prompt silently with the gesture. Students will recognize the gesture and that will cue them.

If you are working on weather, months, days of the week, do this at the same time every day. If you open the lesson with a weather song, play the song every day as part of your routine. Play games and involve the student. Make the game the lesson/session. During the game, pause to ask comprehension questions. If you are working on yes/no questions, then ask yes/no questions! For example, the goal is to ask the student questions beginning with the word "Which" and answer them in complete sentences.

Facilitator: Which color do you want?

Student: Red!

Facilitator: (Refer to the beginning of the sentence starter while providing gestures) "I want the…"

Student: "Red one."

Facilitator: Refer to the beginning, "I …" (Continue to gesture) "I want the…" point or gesture for color.

Student: "I want the red fish."

Facilitator: "Which fishing pole?"

Student: "That one."

Facilitator: "I want the…"

Continue to refer to the whole sentence to add sentence starters, "I like…" or "I want…" etc. When you prompt students, give wait time, limit wording if necessary, give partial words for example: give the sound "r" "re" first when prompting for the word "red." Students will need help positioning their mouths the right way to produce the sound. If you can get a mouth model then you can show exactly where the child needs to position their tongue, how far apart their teeth need to be, etc. Use hand cues for the sound you are making.

Some teachers will do American Sign Language cues or those that will help the students remember the sound. For instance, for the letter 'v', you can hold one hand flat to act like the floor, while two fingers of the other hand are used for the vacuum. When you say "v, vah, vvvvvv" you can act it out and vacuum your hands to provide the cue. This a nonverbal prompt. You can build connections with these gestures and have student act them out as well.

Activities in the Classroom or at Home to Encourage Speech

Cooking or even something like making smoothies can be a great lesson in or out of the classroom. Each child can have a job such as handing out materials, asking each child what they want for the smoothie with visuals. Students can have fun making something they can eat! Make a chart with each students' name on the job they will do in step-by-step order. When it is their turn, they can take their job off the chart (use with Velcro); if not they can simply point to the chart. Although, taking the job will help them have a visual they can bring along with them and place it back when their job is done.

At home, you can create several placemats with cut outs and laminating paper. You may want to laminate at least three times. Make placements for different parts of the day, include conversation pieces, or things to say appropriate for that time such as, "Good morning," "Please pass the___," or "How was your day? Etc."

Do Not Over Prompt Without Modifying First

Sometimes, it is natural to prompt a student again after no response. In education, we save the strongest prompt for last. Minimal and faded prompts is the goal. So, when you are overpromoting and providing children with all the answers, that is okay at the beginning when you are introducing a new goal, but ultimately that is far from mastery. Try to minimize the prompting.

When you are teaching a child how to ride a bicycle, first you start with training wheels, and perhaps you help them push by holding onto the bike itself. However, the goal is not for the child to ride with training wheels. The goal is for the child to ride the bicycle independently without your help. Give ample wait time after your first question and simplify the environment. For me, with 5-minute wait time, the student may get bored and find something else to do. I will wait 1-2 minutes.

For example, when assessing a student for letter identification. It can look something like this:

Facilitator: What letter is this? Circles "b." The

paper has the other 25 letters of the alphabet. Give wait time.

Student: No response

Facilitator: What letter is this? (Points)

Student: No response (Facilitator crosses or cuts out ¼ of the letters.)

Facilitator: What letter is this?

Student: No response (Facilitator crosses or cuts out ½ of the letters.)

Facilitator: What letter is this?

Student: b

Sometimes, students may be too distracted by everything else on the paper. They may be able to read the letter in a group of six, a group of three, or a group of two. Reduce the background clutter in the environment, but also on the paper itself. It is important to keep in mind that students need wait time to process even simple yes or no questions. When you record data, you'll need to write how many prompts and what type of prompt is used to get the child to respond. Then you will take what you know and use it to introduce new concepts.

Chapter 7: Assessments and Lessons

I was one of the classrooms selected for "observation" by an out of state collection of administrators and veteran teachers. However, from what I was told, they only had 12:1:1 class ratio in community schools. They did not have 6:1:1, 8:1:1, 12:1:1 in a specialized school setting. Additionally, I was told they do not believe students with special needs can have the same standards as general education students. Furthermore, they did not share the idea that students with disabilities can be assessed in formal state standardized or alternate assessments with modifications.

I was "voluntold," meaning I wasn't given a choice, as what happens most of the time, to be videotaped with my co-teacher and we discussed our student's data and who we are referring for LRE (Least Restrictive Environment). During this time, I discussed one student who showed progress on the computerized test but did not show any progress on the reading test. The problem was not his decoding skills or fluency. It was his answers on the comprehension portion that did not show growth.

This was a formal assessment, and as part of the nature of the test, students cannot look at visuals. They must illustrate their knowledge with their ability to recall information. This is a standard test for other peers their own age. You are not allowed to alter the test because then it immediately becomes an "informal assessment." In my opinion, this is a big problem, and we cannot accurately assess students if we are so rigid with format. However, as we know, one assessment should not fit all students. Students should be able to illustrate their skills using multiple means of assessment. I believe this should include providing accommodations. On a student's IEP, teachers and therapists must list all accommodations and modifications that a student can use on a test. If it is not listed, then the student is not allowed to use it.

When I implemented this formal reading assessment, there was a book that discussed all the different activities a boy does with his father at the park. After the student reads the story, he/she must answer questions about what he/she read. I modified the assessment and provided visual prompts such as a playground with cartoon children, then another visual with a playground and real children playing, then another visual with simply the playground. In the visual with the playground itself, the student will have to come up with the answer using his/her own experiences with the playground names and activities.

I was told by my superiors that in modifying the assessment, it goes from formal to informal. However, my students were all able to produce more conversation and make more connections having these visuals in front of them. Augmentative speech device works well in my opinion, because speech programs make it possible to isolate vocabulary words to a field of 10, 8, etc. Students can find and choose words from an array of visual aids. By clicking on the word, the speech device speaks to the child and reads aloud. This will also help them make connections kinesthetically, visually, auditorily, and verbally if they can repeat what they hear. However, not all students have a device.

During class, if students are reading an unfamiliar passage and given questions, students may need to use an augmentative speech device, communication board, and be given choices visually to prompt them to produce their best answer. Look back in the text and model your thinking aloud. Illustrate how your conclusion went from Point A to Point B. If the goal is to answer a question beginning with the word "Why?" then you must repeat exercises daily and practice answering that question. Give different examples, settings, visuals, prompt students in the beginning with choices and how they should begin their answer. Students need to practice coming to the same conclusion as you, so you must illustrate and model this with not only words, but with concrete images.

I had a student who was extremely verbal. He was one of the youngest students in my class. In the beginning of the year, he knew few letter sounds, but by the end he was able to read plenty of sight words and simple sentences. He took different assessments. One was computer based where he wore headphones and clicked on one of the multiple choices, and the other is a reading test with a human facilitator. From his computerized test, you may have thought he regressed in reading when it was exactly the opposite. The time he took on the test showed he spent 18 minutes to answer 40 questions. He rapidly clicked.

This test did not illustrate that growth, only the paper-based reading test showed growth. So not all assessments work well for students. By March, he moved from a reading level of AA level to an instructional C level, and independent B according to the reading assessment. In comparison to other students his age (Kindergarten) in a sense, he caught up to his peers in the general education. He was exactly where he needed to be for reading and math. He came in every day with the drive to learn. He came from a single parent household, and his mother did not like the idea of doing a lot of homework because she had other kids to take care of. I worried that he would quickly regress but I referred him to ICT, or Inclusive Classroom Teaching. The goal is to aim students for a least restrictive environment, and every year staff and parents should come to an agreement that would benefit the child the most.

A student's learning does not end at the end of the school day; he/she should be given opportunities beyond that. Students with special needs may have a different learning style than their general ed peers but do have the potential to be appropriately challenged according to their age, using the right framework. To make my students successful, I outlined a consistent schedule with rotating centers that involved kinesthetic, visual, verbal, and auditory aspects. I incorporate music into every subject they were learning. I would read their physical energy and provide sensory breaks when needed. I would give frustration toys at certain points of the day and provide vibrating or weighted and therapeutic objects which would help them relief stress and anxiety. Maintaining a positive and efficient classroom environment also means maintaining a healthy equilibrium, that includes a physical, and social-emotional connections too.

Following a consistent schedule made the students feel comfortable very quickly. At the beginning of each instructional period, I discuss everything that we are going to do from start to finish. Then, we go through each step-by-step. Then, I will remind them of the step that comes after as I am following the procedure, even if we do this daily. For our math period, after a mini-lesson, we work on our workbook pages using different manipulatives at each table. Students will raise their hands to pass out the pencils. When it is time to do work at our tables, they may stand up to do their work; they may move in their chair while doing it. We use highlighted markers to provide visual cues to show them where to right. We may underline the space or draw a box where we want them to write.

Morning Meeting

Create a morning routine that is short and consistent. During my morning meeting, I review the date, day of the week, month, and year. I go over any event happening in the week. I like to give the students days, if not weeks' notice, prior to that event. I will go over the schedule of the day and classroom expectations using visuals. I will ask them, "What did you do over the weekend? Did you play games? Did you go to the park?" If their parents send me pictures of activities, they've done then I will show them to the class, and we will discuss it.

One of my students likes to go to Target with his dad. I asked him, "Did you go to Target with your dad?" I will give opportunities for conversation. The morning meeting sets the tone for the day. Each student will express how they are feeling by placing their name or portrait on the face or word which illustrates their feeling the best. We end our morning meeting with a song, and each student will play an instrument. Then I will give out points to each student, and transition into the next subject area.

Some Ideas to Keep in Mind While Teaching the Alphabet

Learning letter identification and letter sounds are learned with a variety of meaningful experiences. When assigning daily worksheets, warm up, or homework, make sure that students can illustrate their knowledge in different ways. For example, have students circle, cut and paste, rainbow write (trace letters with different colored crayons), and provide opportunities for students to copy letters onto paper with visual highlighted cues, and dry/erase white boards.

If the student is having difficulty, consider working on one line at a time, for example. First, the student can make horizontal lines, then vertical lines the following week (or until mastery with horizontal); afterward, the student can work on crossing both lines together. Use visual highlighted cues to show students where they begin. Visual highlighted cues can be an actual line that they trace, or a box they have to write the letter in, or perhaps you are underlining the lines on the notebook with small dashes, or dots. By giving visuals, you are also directing letter size and spacing. For example, a small box, or short line would mean a small letter goes there. As part of learning through sensory opportunities, if you are using flash cards each day for a warm-up that lasts several minutes, consider making the letters texturized so that students can run their fingers across bumps and ridges as they are repeating the letter name and/or sound. Use Play-Doh, shaving cream, or paint to mold letters, and have students engage and practice working with different materials. This also helps their fine motor skills and hand-eye coordination.

Incorporate creative poster ideas, felt activities, laminate letters and pictures then stick-on magnets for repeated use. Students can make letter puppets, letter paper hats, and act out the sound/ letter names. Incorporate music and movement with learning. Can students clap out letter names and sounds? Can they use sign language or sky write, or trace their fingers on the carpet in the shape of the letter? Sometimes, when I'd put on a song for a specific letter, the students may remember the catchy beat and start picking up on the words of the song.

Before you begin teaching letters, remember to take a baseline assessment with the date and write down accommodations you have used. If you are asking the child to identify letters in a field of 20, 10, or 5 make sure you write that in. If a student cannot identify a letter in a field of 20, move down to 15 then 10, and so on. Remember to give ample wait time before prompting again. If a student does not respond right away, it does not always mean he/she doesn't know the answer. Try giving him/her wait time to process the question; you can ask in fewer words and make the field of letters smaller.

Learning Sight Words

Sight words are learned with daily repetition. If you are going to read a book to the whole class, consider reviewing vocabulary words and sight words prior to reading. Make sight words a part of a mini-lesson or daily skill-based centers. Students can mold clay/dough into sight word mats, stencils, or play tools. You can have students paint, use shaving cream to write words, cut and paste, and glue rice or pasta to construction paper to form a sight word.

There are tons of sensory related activities for students to do that create meaningful experiences and connections to learning. Make a communication board with symbols to match each word. You can even cut the words and make a word ring. Break up the class into three tiers, and each group can get sight words according to their level. I go over sight words and letter sounds at the beginning of each phonics lesson as a review/ warm up.

As students learn sight words, continue with your ongoing assessments, and refer back to your baseline assessment to see if progress is being made and what words the students still have trouble with and where you can move on. Have students test other peers, and provide feedback. You can make a communication board with the question and answers they will need to recite.

Comprehension Questions

Communication boards are versatile in literacy. So, as you are reading a story, students can follow along with a communication board for quick visual cues. When we read a story, oftentimes we find it hard to relate to characters because they are not like us.

Here are some things to keep in mind when teaching literacy and focusing on comprehension questions that begin with "Who, What, When, Where, Why or How?" Perhaps, it is also an IEP communication goal. For instance, if you are working on asking "What" questions (example, "What animal is that? What color is the boy's shirt?"), then that will be our focus when we do read-alouds and small group instruction.

Let's say the student has mastered "What" questions; now you want to move onto "Who and Where," (for example, "Who is that? Who is speaking? Who is next to the girl? Or "Where are the kids playing? Where is he going?) You can also move onto "When" questions such as "When did he wake up? When is she going to eat lunch? When is he going to sleep?") The questions that require more abstract thinking are the "Why" and "How" questions. Save these for last until the student has mastered the "What, Who, When and Where" questions.

When I am practicing comprehension questions, I make an adapted book of the story I am focusing on for reading. The book includes simpler sentences, that are more concrete. So, they may include less dialogue and are more to the point of what is being expressed on the page. However, I will also use the original text. The original text should preferably include enlarged text and visuals. This will make it easier to point to text and visuals.

I use a communication board which is usually a 5 x 4 array of small visuals with labels. The communication board is essentially used as a reference for you and the child as he/she reads. In my experience, it helps keep them engaged and connected to the story from beginning to the middle, and end. During or after you read, take out your comprehension questions that you want to work on. I print and laminate my comprehension questions then place them all on a key ring.

Comprehension questions should have the question and 2-3 choices for an answer with visuals for each answer. If a question has multiple answers, then edit the answer selection to include both answers. For example, if the question is "What is the setting of the story?" The setting is a specific question because it is only found at the beginning of the story. However, it requires multiple answers. The setting means the time the story starts, such as daytime, afternoon or evening. It also includes the place where the story began. So, let us say the setting is during the day, on a farm. One answer selection can show a picture of a farm with a nighttime sky/ moon, another selection can be at the zoo during the day, and another selection can show a picture of a sun shining down on a farm to represent during the day on a farm. So, the correct choice would be the last. The first choice provided half of the correct answer, which was the farm, but the time was wrong. If you want to pay a little more attention to place, then you can choose to take out the farm for that visual and make two different places entirely for your answer selections.

In addition to comprehension questions, and a communication board, I also make sequencing boards. It is a similar concept to the communication board, but it can be fewer visuals or even more. I will make three sequencing boards. The first is the beginning of the story, the second is the middle, and the third is the end of the story. I will make simple sentences in the form of 1-2 rows. Each word in the sentence will have its own visual. Students can point to each word and read it. I can ask questions like, "What happened in the beginning of the story? What did she do? Who did she meet?" They can point and answer using their sequencing boards.

As an extension, have students act out the story with puppets. Facilitate actions and dialogue as you move along. You can use a felt board or magnets with a white board. You can make your own felt board by stapling a large piece of black felt onto a cardboard cutout. After you print visuals, cut them out, laminate and either stick magnets to the back or a piece of Velcro, depending on what board you are using. Students can play with these puppets in a small group center or choice time.

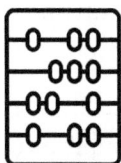

Tips In Teaching Pre-Math Readiness Skills

My students love using math manipulatives for learning through play. They like to stack and connect cubes, blocks, and use counting bears and counters. They get a feel for math and without realizing it they are counting, adding, and subtracting.

During whole group instruction, students will have a number chart in front of them along with a number line. If a student cannot count past five then I will have a number chart from 0-10, If a student cannot count past 15 then the chart will go up to 20, and so on. In my experience, the students find it hard to point and keep up with a guided lesson because they are overwhelmed by a sea of numbers. So I gradually increase the resource content that they are exposed to. When teaching number identification and counting, aside from numbers, I provide visuals in the form of words, dots, and real-life pictures to represent a number. I print and laminate pictures of the manipulatives the students like to use such as connecting cubes and I attach sticky magnets so that I can use them on the white board. Then, I will do a mini-lesson illustrating several problems with these.

I attach Velcro™ to my counters and add magnets to arrays to use for whole or small group instruction. I will use real materials such as crayons, markers, and even snacks to illustrate a problem. It also makes math more relatable to them. Have students stand up and take turns going to the board to solve math problems.

When reading a math related book, illustrate the problem so they can see it. Students need visuals and opportunities to engage in some way. They cannot solely listen to you lecture or read from a book.

Naptime

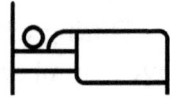

Some questions to think about:

➢ How do you want this to look?
➢ What ambience would you want to have to take a nap?

If there is relaxing music that you'd like to play, then playing it frequently will signal it's time to relax (auditory cue.) In class, after turning on the smartboard, I would walk over to turn off the lights. Every time I did it the same way. The smartboard goes on and I would walk over to turn on the lights. So, one day after I turned on the smartboard, one of my students jumped up out of his seat to turn off the lights. I allowed this to be his job. I would turn on the smartboard, and he would get up like clockwork. He would know exactly what I was going to do, and I didn't have to say a word. If they are verbal, they can remind you what you are forgetting. For them, a routine is like completing a puzzle and all you have left is one piece, but it is no-where to be found. If something is missing from the routine/ puzzle, it can be frustrating.

During naptime try to create a less stimulating en-vironment. A white poster board can be helpful here and should be placed on a flat surface beside the stu-dent's upper body to create a less stimulating environ-ment. This can help them to relax. A weighted blanket or toy can provide added pressure and relaxation.

When I was a student-teacher in a Pre-k 6:1:1 class, there was a student who could not sleep during nap-time unless there was a weight on him. He had his weighted alligator toy beside him in his cot. A white three-fold poster board was placed behind his head to reduce stimuli. After several minutes, he fell into a very deep sleep and did not want to wake up after-ward. When speaking with the student's mother, she relayed that she uses her leg as a weight. She demon-strated this by placing one leg across the boy's stom-ach/legs. With this, he was able to relax from feeling the weight from his mother's leg. To help with sleep-ing, there are also weighted blankets. Sometimes, stu-dents with high hyperactivity need to feel that weight to help them relax before sleeping. Students may need pressure, and sensory input to help them relax.

Stephanie L. Lindner

Collaborating With Parents, Administration, and Other Staff

In my experience, parents appreciate transparent communication. Most new parents and new teachers know very little about autism if they do not have prior experience, unless they have a relative or an older child with autism and are new to managing classic behaviors associated. Additionally, it is common for students with autism to have multiple disabilities including speech deficit disorder, deaf and blindness, ADHD, etc.

Students with autism and other disabilities need their parents and teachers to collaborate to find the best modifications/ accommodations for them to learn in and out of the classroom. This will take trial and error and the willingness to think outside the box and to try different things. It can be the end of the school year and I am still collaborating with the speech therapist, counselor, parent, and occupational therapist discussing one student, updating his/her modifications/ accommodations. Students need to be appropriately challenged and rewarded. Collaborating is all year long.

In collaborating with parents, I always found it useful to do mass emails or message via online platform. I like monthly newsletters that discuss what skills you are working on in the classroom, and how parents can help at home. Set a blank box aside in the newsletter so you can customize the newsletter and write down what their child has been really good at for that particular month, for example, "John has been helpful in helping organize the classroom library. Jane has been transitioning into math with ease and is so excited when we sing our number song."

Communication may be difficult at times, depending on administration. When I worked in the city, admin wanted complete control over everything, and teachers were micro-managed. When I moved outside into the suburbs, it was the total opposite. Less micromanagement, and in turn more communication with parents, and colleagues. The tone was also more positive, supportive, and trusting overall. You don't realize how toxic a work environment can be until you finally leave it and find something better.

In the city, perhaps, placing such strict rules makes it easier for them to monitor and this may work for some people. In the city, I had to document the time, and what we spoke about, and the messages online are read by several staff members, including the principal. I know this because I was asked about a "private conversation" that I had with a parent. It was solely through messaging. I was also told on more than one occasion to make sure my messages were not "too long." This kind of deterred me from providing more parent communication. It made me want to communicate with parents less and avoid communication altogether if I could help it. Phone conversations via cellphone are frowned upon because then anyone can call you after work hours.

There are a lot of restrictions in how a teacher is permitted to speak, so much so that it creates insecurity, and oftentimes after a conversation with a parent, I'd obsess over information that was said. Oftentimes, I stuck to the facts and never shared any hint of my personality. I find this to be challenging at times, because parents may directly ask me for my opinion and want my guidance on personal matters with their child at home. Some parents feel alone and need someone to confide in.

When I worked in the city, I could relate speaking to parents and administration to much like walking on eggshells. I would have taken eggshells any day if given the choice. In the city, the perspective of administration is much like a police officer; anything a teacher says will be used against them. Therefore, we must be on constant guard not to come off so candid and informal. When I moved to the suburbs, my principal was much more personable and supportive in every way. I felt that I was not just an employee but a person of value. So, it made coming to work entirely different. I didn't feel like it was work, but something I wanted to do and received enjoyment from. This new attitude helped my teaching, and brough a positive change from within.

My advice to new teachers, is to make a personal notebook with anecdotes on everything you do, including your conversations with parents with times and dates. Be transparent with administration, but always, always professional, and respectful. When I worked as a teacher's assistant in pre-k, I observed parents coming in often and assisting with arts and craft projects, reading a book aloud during whole group instruction, and coming in with homemade food to celebrate a multi-cultural holiday with an abundance of cheer and smiles. This is how harmoniously involved parents were, but this takes communication and agreement with administration all around. Parents, teachers, and administrators should not be against one another, but they should come together for the sake of their child out of respect for one another. The kids benefit from it in the end.

If parents are quiet and have not reached out to you at all—reach out to them. I will schedule times in the week to communicate with most parents about anything. Call parents for good news—not just bad. During my conversations, I ask questions about the child and talk about my notices/ wonderings and parents really like how interested I am in their child. This helps our relationship. Parents may be nervous of new teachers, so I try to give them as much information as possible and let them know I am here to clarify any concerns and questions they may have. I am here to support them.

Using Paraprofessionals To Help With Routines

Each morning, my paraprofessionals and I make sure the students come in with labels on all their belongings. In my experience, students' belongings can easily get mixed up and if he/she goes home without their own clothes, even accidentally, parents can be really upset which is understandable. What ends up happening is that students' belongings can fall and be picked up and placed on another hook. In a classroom where the students have uniforms, a sweater could look the same if it's not labeled. Make sure everything is labeled as the students come in to unpack. If there are items that are not labeled, be sure to label them. I get a pack of fabric labels and by the end of the month about half are used. Be clear of your arrival and dismissal routine with your paraprofessionals and try to set aside a space for each student to prevent disorganization. If you are relying on your paraprofessionals to keep the students organized, and they go home, and this does not seem like the case—it will always fall on you even if it is not. As a teacher be prepared to be everywhere at once. It is not that you don't trust others to carry out their responsibilities—it just that you know little mistakes can happen, we make them all the time—we're human. Oversee as much as you can at arrival and dismissal. If your paraprofessional picks up a student from the main office, and has a conversation with the parent, make sure they let you know everything that was talked about and make a mental note, document in your anecdotes if you can.

At the beginning of the year, make your expectations known to your paraprofessionals. This is part of being a teacher, knowing when and how to delegate responsibilities to your classroom team. They need to know what their job is and what you expect them to do. This also will make their life easier. If one of their responsibilities is to sharpen pencils or organize the library, then they can work this into their day. It makes the classroom structure more consistent. Try and talk about things outside the work environment, and if you feel comfortable. It my experience, it has made work much more pleasant when you feel like you connect with your team.

Trips

During morning meeting, when I usually go over the schedule for the day, I will discuss the trip, where we are going, what we will see, and which chaperones are going with us. I will go over the rules and what we must do while crossing the street, how they are expected to line up, sit down on the bus etc. Even if they have heard the rules at least a hundred times, I will still go over them as if they did not already know. I will show students pictures of where we are going on the smartboard. I will organize chaperones and student groupings. I will try to pair one student that has high needs with another that is the opposite, so they usually balance each other out. I will refrain from putting two or three students with high needs in one group. I will try to push parents to go so that they can watch their child on the trip and maybe even their child's friend. I mainly teach K-3, so I will often have the chaperones hold hands while we are walking from place to place. Since we are a city school, the trips are also in the city, so it is always crowded wherever we go. We make sure that they are not too far so that we may leave and come back before dismissal time. Before we leave, I write down a description of what each child is wearing, I include the brand and color of the clothes. The students wear nametags that have their names, parents' names, my name and their address and phone number. I print, laminate, and attach them to a lanyard. Also, on the lanyard I will attach fidget toys, otherwise what will end up happening is the students will play and rip the actual nametags. These fidget toys come in handy during transitions. I noticed the students may twiddle them in their hands or bite them out of nervousness. The students must wear these nametags the entire time. If the students keep taking them off and tossing them, then I usually attach the tag to a belt loop on their jeans. Make sure the students all use the bathroom. Bring wipes, extra diapers, and hand sanitizer. I also carry an EpiPen as I am trained to use it if I have a student highly allergic to something. During the trip I will often stop and do a head count of my students to make sure they are all there. If I have chaperones, I make sure I have their phone number in the event we are somehow separated. During lunch, I will try to squeeze my students to sit in one area, so they are not spread out with the public. This makes it easier to keep an eye on them. I take pictures so that we can review and discuss them in the classroom afterward. After lunch, all students use the bathroom. If I have a male paraprofessional, then he will take the boys to the bathroom. If not, I will try to borrow one from another class while I watch their students. We are all team players, so we often figure this part out quickly without issues. Do head counts before and after lunch and before boarding the bus to go back to school.

School Events

During morning meeting, I will mention the school event two weeks prior and daily leading up to the day of and discuss details. I will also discuss the rules of the auditorium and behavior expectations. I will also mention the token economy system, so the students realize that rewards do not cease. You can show a video of a performance and show visuals, "Ok what does a good audience member do? How do they act?" Show a visual for a calm body, and quiet mouth, etc." Practice if you need to, and practice how students should line up, exit the room, and sit in their seats. Before going to the event, do something that requires exercise in the classroom. Encourage the students to break of sweat especially if they are just going to sit and watch as audience members for a long period afterward. This way they would have come from an active and engaging activity and are more likely to relax and sit down with other classes. If I have a student that is sensitive to noise to the point they try to escape, cry or meltdown then I will bring noise canceling headphones, and the fidget toys they like. Use the fidget toys that they don't normally have access to daily, so that when they do have it, they will be actively engaged in it. Most of the time, students will easily get bored with the school event especially if it is hours long. For any student, it is challenging to sit and watch a presentation that is hours long. I will bring several other fidget toys and rotate them around. Before handing the fidget toys, I will make my behavioral expectations clear. If students are not sitting or are engaging in a nonpreferred behavior, then I will go over what I want them to do instead then once they change their behavior, I will hand them the toy. Do a headcount before leaving classroom, during transitioning in the hallway, before you sit down in the auditorium and before leaving the auditorium. In fact, if there are a lot of people, and students walking back and forth do it as many times as you need. Students can easily sneak into another line, class, etc. if there are not enough people to watch them. It can be for a bathroom break or simply because they are tired of sitting. When you come back into the classroom, provide feedback, and engage in your token economy system.

Chapter 8: Writing the IEP

At the beginning of the school year, you must be familiar with the IEP (Individualized Education Plan) and the student's goals, including accommodations and modifications. Make yourself known to the students' therapists and counselors. If you begin to see that a student never got the services listed in "recommended services" or are missing days, then make a note of this. I had a sign-in sheet for the service providers where they would sign out a student with the time and date. This way, I was able to keep a record of their sessions but also it was a way for me to see which students were absent and how much therapy they missed. If a student is constantly missing therapy, he/she may not get the most out of their academic day. Speech can have a positive impact in promoting participation in multi-subjects. Occupational therapy and physical therapy can help students complete classwork and engage in activities. Counseling can help peer to peer relationships, etc. If a student is often absent, then this is something that should be brought up by the team during the IEP meeting.

As you assess throughout the year, you should also keep track on IEP goal progress monitoring to determine which goals you need to continue to work on, and which goals the student has mastered. Before the IEP meeting, I will do a phone conference with the parent to discuss the student's behavior in class, and the progress they have made thus far. If there is a certain behavior that needs to be addressed, do not wait for the IEP meeting to bring it up. The parents should have a general idea of what is going on in class before the meeting. It should not be the first time they are hearing important information related to behavior. If not, then the parent may be upset that you have withheld any important information, especially pertaining to behavior. They may say something like "I had no idea this was going on in class." Now you do not have to go over each goal during the phone conference but take care to go over general topics like reading, writing, math, behavior in class, etc. Have open lines of communication prior to the IEP meeting. The parent should already have an idea of how their child is doing in class thus far, this should not be all new information. Parents need to take an active approach in their child's schooling. Essentially, they are also the teacher, they are the home teacher and the one that is with the child the most.

During the IEP meeting, review the student's assessment scores and the grade equivalent for each subject. Then review IEP goals and be specific as possible as to why the student needs more time to master the goal. In addition, I like to go over some things the parents can do to help at home. Again, collaboration is key to ensure progress has been made all around. Afterward, review the recommended services, accommodations for next year.

The IEP includes information pertaining to the student, their strengths, areas of concern, interests, and preferences. It includes statements that are not based on opinion. The information is based off careful observational data, and formal assessments. Statements pertaining to academics, and behavior are objective and based on evidence. IEPs will look different state to state so I will not discuss a specific format but will instead go over general topics. In the IEP itself you want to address all areas such as: activities of daily living, levels of intellectual functioning, and adaptive behavior, social-emotional development, and physical development.

In the activities of daily living, you will want to discuss your observations on personal care. Here are some examples of the type of information you may want to include. I'm no expert in writing the IEP, but I will share how I would personally approach it. The best way for me to go about this is to come up with examples using fake students, John and Jane. You'll want to be as concrete and literal as possible when sharing your observations. For each of these impact statements you should say the type and number of prompting beforehand. For example "With 1-2 verbal prompts...Jane can..." or "With 3-5 verbal and visual cues...John can...

Let's begin,

For activities of daily living, according to recorded teacher observations...

- With a maximum of 2 verbal prompts, John can walk to the bathroom independently and manage his clothes to use the toilet. He can take soap from the soap dispenser to wash his hands and dry his hands with a paper towel.

- Upon entering the classroom, John can take off his coat and hang it on his assigned hook, with 1-2 verbal prompts he can place his lunch bag in lunch/snack bin. During lunchtime, John can spear his food with a fork, and scoop his applesauce with a spoon independently.

- Jane needs hand over hand assistance from a female paraprofessional to unbutton her clothing before using the toilet. She needs 1-2 verbal cues to take soap from the soap dispenser, lather and wash her hands, and get a paper towel.

- During lunch time, Jane requires hand over hand support in opening her Tupperware from home. In the area of household activities, when coming into the classroom, Jane needs hand over hand support, to unzip her coat and lift her bookbag on her hook under her picture tag.

- Upon entering the classroom John smiles and greets his fellow peers by waving his hand independently. John follows two-step verbal directives and walks to the student center area to take a pencil and retrieve his math notebook from his bin.

- Based on recorded teacher observations, John performs well in class. John can follow 1-2 step verbal instructions and he expresses his ideas primarily via verbal means.

- Jane follows one-step directives and requires a visual schedule to perform activities throughout the school day. Jane says "Hello" upon entering the classroom given 1-2 verbal prompts. Jane follows 1-step directives and expresses her ideas primarily via her AAC (augmentative and alternative communication) device.

In the areas of cognitive or academic performance in reading, writing and math, discuss the title of the assessment data, when it was given, and what the assessment results mean. If appropriate compare his/her results to the beginning of the year, if there is progress then this should be something you highlight first before going into what the student is struggling with. Here is an example of what this may look like:(Name) was given an assessment on (date, year.)

- In the area of reading, according to (name of assessment), (name of student) received a score of __. The national norm in relation to his peers is ___. According to these results, as well as curriculum assessments, and recorded teacher observations given verbal and physical prompts, John presents the ability to understand the prepositional words "in" and "on", and can distinguish between real and make-believe characters, as well as recognize characters from a familiar literary book. John can identify colors (list the colors), school supplies (name several supplies he can label) and food with his symbol-based communication book, as well as answer yes or no questions by pointing. John can match lowercase and uppercase letters from A-Z. Additionally, John can distinguish between lowercase and uppercase letters.

You can go into more depth when it comes to specific skills. An example can be: (Name) can decode cvc and cvce (consonant vowel consonant and consonant vowel consonant silent e) words with long vowel sounds. (Name) can decode cvc and cvce words with long vowel sounds. You must also write down the areas of need in each subject, while again, being as specific as possible.

- For example: Areas of need are decoding cvc and cvce words including word families at, an, it, ip, et and en. Additionally, he needs support in answering reading comprehension questions with "where" and "who" in a fictional text pertaining to characters, setting and plot.
- In the area of math, according to (name of assessment) results John received a score of ___. The national norm in comparison with peers his own age is___. According to, curriculum assessments, and teacher observations,

John presented the ability to classify a given object from the environment as a circle or triangle, and match the names of shapes to given 2-D shape visuals using teacher made materials. Additionally, John can count out a given number of objects within 10 and can compare sets of objects using the term "most."

More examples include:

- Given 1-2 verbal prompts, Jane is able to match 3D shapes in file folder activities, she's also able to identify them by pointing to correct 3D shape in a field of 9.
- Given 1-2 verbal prompts, John can count by 1's within 100, identify the last object in a group or line. John can identify a given number when by pointing in a field of 10.
- In horizontal and vertical format, John can solve addition problems with sums 10-20, and subtract numbers with differences up to 10 given a maximum of 2 verbal and visual prompts.
- Areas of need are comparing numbers 0-20, understanding math vocabulary words such as "less than, greater than, and equal to/ same number."

In the area of writing/language use, according to curriculum assessments, and teacher observations, John presented the ability to trace lowercase letters a-z and copy letters from a model.

- Jane can color and cut paper and paste in appropriate area, she can copy words from a model but requires visual highlighted prompts such as box or line to direct where to write and help with letter sizing and spacing.

- Areas of need include support in writing on the line, with appropriate letter size and spacing. John needs support in knowing when to capitalize a letter and sequence 1-3 visual events and using the words "First, Then/Next, Last".

- In the area of communication, given 3-5 verbal prompts, Jane presented the ability to speak in 5–7-word sentences, turn take with a peer, express her wants/needs and request, express different emotions and raise her hand to participate in whole group activities.

- Joe can sequence 1-3 events of a story given 1-2 verbal prompts, but has difficulty explaining what happened in complete sentences. Joe can state the main idea of the story but needs prompting and support in including supporting details of a story. Joe can answer why questions using pictures/ symbol format pertaining to a read aloud.

- Areas of need in communication are speaking in 3–4-word sentences using verbal prompts and turn-take during whole group (12 students) instruction and engage with peers (It's your turn (student's name) and wait his turn for 3-5 minutes.

In the levels of adaptive behavior discuss how the student can navigate and adapt in his/her environment, and how he/she responds to classroom rules, transitions, change in schedule, etc.

- John presents as a cooperative child when engaging in a preferred task. He attends to tasks with 3-5 visual, verbal, and physical prompts. John can transition calmly from the classroom to the cafeteria given visual cue cards. John maintains appropriate eye contact with whole group (12 students), small group (3-4) and 1:1 instruction and demonstrates joint attention and joint action during choice time activities. John will verbally say "I need help" when he needs help with classwork or is putting on his clothes and buttoning his jacket or opening his snack.

There will most likely be some sort of social-emotional section expanding on behavior. This section will expand the student's relationship with peers and adults, how the student handles stressful situations, and any interventions that have worked for the student such as a token economy system (points, sticker chart, etc.) and strategies that he/she engages in such as breathing techniques, etc.

Here is an example of what it may look like:

- Jane is a 6-year-old girl. She will smile and use words to express wants/ needs, "I want…". Jane can sit independently at an appropriate distance from her peers while sitting in whole (12 students) and small groups (3-4 students.) Jane participates in classroom activities using 3-4 verbal prompts. She can initiate conversations with peers and adults by asking "Wh" questions, "What are you doing?" "Where is the doll?" "When is lunch?" During lunch, she can sit next to other students and eat her snacks.

- According to teacher observations, John can follow daily routines provided with 1-2 verbal prompts, and minimal assistance. John will often raise his hand to volunteer for classroom jobs and answer questions on the smartboard during whole group instruction. During morning instruction, given 1-2 verbal prompts "How do you feel?" oftentimes he verbally states, "I feel good." When he is verbally prompted, John can take a musical instrument and participate in singing and playing music. During transitions, John needs 1-2 verbal prompts to stay in line with the class and navigate the school building. John needs 1-2 verbal prompts per 50-minute instructional period to stay on task, listen with ears, look with eyes, and sit in his assigned area.

Observational data is collected daily. John participates (name intervention or token economy system.) Each 50-minute period he and his classmates are able to earn 5 points. One point for ___ (discuss each point.) The class tracks points throughout the school day using (method.) John's points are used to determine what special activities are earned, such as choice time and insert other activities. Choice time includes IEP skill-based games and activities aligned with grade appropriate Common Core Standards. John's current individualized behavior goal is to keep calm and wait for his turn. When participating in a group activity, John will cry continuously and shout "No!" when he is not chosen. As a result, he will walk to the classroom calm down area and engage in calm down techniques which involve deep breathing and counting 0-10. Afterward, he will rejoin his class to complete the task at hand. The goal is to help John have more self-control with his body when he displays frustration with differentiated instruction. John needs support in waiting at least 3-5 minutes for his turn and allowing his peers to have turns as well.

The physical mobility section is typically filled out by a physical therapist. However, not all students have physical therapy. So here's an example of what you may want to include:

- School Mobility/Transitions: John is able to walk with his peers in the hallway. He can follow directions or 1-2 verbal cues to stay in line. He can manage flights of stairs in the school building at the same pace as his class-mates. He walks with alternating/ step-over-step pattern in going up and down the stairs. John can transition with 1-2 verbal prompts to the bathroom, gym, cafeteria, or different levels of the school building with adult supervision. Upon receiving 1-2 verbal and visual prompts, he can push open doors, turn handles, and pull the door to open.

- Arrival/Dismissal/Busing: John goes to school on a school bus. He can get and on and off the bus with 1-2 physical prompts. He holds on to the handrail for support with 1-2 verbal prompts. John can transition from the bus to his classroom each morning independently with adult supervision. John can transition from his bus to his classroom. Each afternoon he can transition to his assigned room for busing and to his school bus independently with staff su-pervision.

- Bathroom/Toileting: John can tell staff when if he needs to go to the bathroom sponta-neously. He can manage his clothes inde-pendently. He needs 1-2 verbal prompts to turn the faucet on and off and use the soap dis-penser.

- Mealtime/Snack Time: John can receive his tray/food items during lunch. He can feed himself independently using a fork. He needed some hand-over-hand assistance with opening his snack or a carton of milk or juice. With minimal prompting, John is able to clean up and throw remaining contents into the garbage bin.

In the IEP you will include recommended modifications and accommodations. All special education students should have something. Here are examples of what may be included: individualized daily visual schedule, preferential seating, use of aids/assistive technology: dynamic display speech generating device, tests read: test passages, questions, items, and multiple choice responses read by a human reader to the student for all tests, manipulatives, graphic organizers, modeling, vocabulary cues, positive behavior reminds, verbal redirection, transition cues, adapted books, adapted school supplies including pencil grips, repetitions, etc.

The IEP essentially gives a window view of the child to the next support service team, this includes the special education teacher and the therapists that the student receives. The information needs to be objective, and specific. The IEP needs to cover all areas of strengths and areas of concern. Include parental concerns in academics, social and physical areas. Write *verbatim* what the parent has said regarding concerns for the child from the IEP meeting. The recommended services also need to be discussed and parents need to agree or reject next year's services. During the meeting, if age appropriate, you will need to discuss if the student is doing state or alternative testing and what accommodations he/she will receive, and whether he/she will continue to receive services in the summer months. You will need to discuss classroom and bus accommodations as well. As in the IEP itself, refrain from opinionated statements and only speak objectively according to your observations. The parent, however, is obviously allowed to make opinionated statements regarding their child.

Final Note

When I first started teaching, I was scared and felt extremely unprepared. You can try your best to be the perfect teacher, or perfect parent. In your mind, you may have a picture of who that would be. Give yourself a break, nobody is perfect and if it seems like they are—just realize you only get to see one side of them. We don't know the experiences that person has had, and led them to do what they do. As you teach, you'll discover your own teaching style, you'll grow more confident. Teaching requires dedication and patience to help students reach their fullest potential. It is a rich and rewarding experience to help students learn, as a parent or teacher. Learning to read, write, count, and communicate is something that you can't put a price tag on. We have the power to make everything an opportunity for learning, and it takes persistence, time, and inspiration from you. Be an inspiration to your students by modeling the best version of yourself. It's hard when life happens, and you must always take care of yourself—practice self-care, think kind thoughts. If you mess up and make a mistake during an observation, think of what you would say to yourself if you were someone else. You can write a long list of accommodations but remember that you are the most powerful tool in teaching students. Don't let technicalities, insurmountable paperwork, and bad attitudes from others cloud your vision of being the best. Give yourself hugs and breathe in and out. Pace yourself and don't forget to provide some positive reinforcement as well. For the most success, remember to work as a team even if that teams is only two people. It is my hope that this guidebook serves as a first step into mentoring new teachers and parents with children that have disabilities, who want extra support at home. Remember, you are not alone.

About The Author

Stephanie Lindner has worked in the field of education for over a decade. She received an M.S. in special education and early childhood education from the City University of New York at Lehman College. She currently works as a special education teacher for the New Milford Public Schools District. She enjoys spending time with her family, and lives with her husband and their son in Connecticut.